DE PROPRIETATIBUS LITTERARUM

edenda curat

C. H. VAN SCHOONEVELD

Indiana University

Series Practica, 2

D1481526

THE REALISM

OF

DREAM VISIONS

The Poetic Exploitation of the Dream-Experience
in Chaucer and his Contemporaries

by

CONSTANCE B. HIEATT
St. John's University

1967
MOUTON & CO.
THE HAGUE · PARIS

Printed in The Netherlands by Mouton & Co., Printers, The Hague.

PREFACE

The germ of this study was an examination of Chaucer's dream visions written under the primary direction of Professor Helaine Newstead, of Hunter College of the City University of New York, who first planted the idea in my mind. Professor E. Talbot Donaldson of Yale University guided me in further work on Middle English dream visions. It was with his encouragement that I embarked on a dissertation on the subject. For help at that stage, I am also particularly indebted to Professor John C. Pope. The dissertation was accepted by the Yale Graduate School in 1959.

The present book is a recasting of the dissertation. In preparing it for publication, I have tried to benefit from all the comments and criticisms made by various scholars and colleagues – not least, of course, my husband, Professor A. Kent Hieatt, of Columbia University. My apologies are due to those whose suggestions I have not entirely followed. I am solely responsible for any flaws or infelicities which remain in this final version.

Portions of Chapters 5 and 8 have appeared in *Studia Neophilologica* and *American Notes and Queries*. I am grateful to the editors for permission to use this material.

Among the many other teachers, colleagues, and friends who have helped me at various stages and in various ways, I owe special thanks to Professor Muriel Bowden, under whom I studied Chaucer as an undergraduate; the late Professors Marjorie Anderson and Helge Kökeritz, two of the scholars of Old and Middle English with whom it was my good fortune to study; and Dr. Frank A. Wolff, who read my chapter on modern dream psychology.

CONTENTS

INTRODUCTION

One of the more popular poetic forms in fourteenth and fifteenth century England was the dream vision; some of the most important of the
great fourteenth century Middle English poems are cast in this form,
and its influence is to be found in almost all the poets of the fifteenth
century, whether or not they were actually writing poems which techni-
cally meet the definition of a "dream vision". On the continent the
heyday of the dream vision was somewhat earlier, but there too it was,
in its time, one of the most popular forms of medieval poetry.

Today the dream vision has almost entirely disappeared; many
readers of poetry would not have any clear idea of what the term
means at all. John Livingston Lowes said of the dream form that it
was half-dead in Chaucer's day and is dead now a second time.[1] This
is, of course, true only of the allegorical dream vision of the specifically
medieval type; that dreams as a literary form are still with us should
be obvious to readers of *Finnegans Wake*. But the form used by
Chaucer, Langland, and the *Pearl*-poet, among a great many others,
certainly seems a little strange today, and the question remains: why
did medieval poets so frequently prefer to cast their works into the
form of a dream? Did the dream form have characteristics and advan-
tages which made it particularly attractive to poets of this period?

It hardly seems a sufficient explanation to attribute it all to imitation
of the *Romance of the Rose,* or to slavish following of "convention".
This would not tell us why the form was sufficiently popular to become
a convention, or why a poet might have chosen to write any one particular poem within the convention. In the case of *Pearl*, for example,
if we accept the theory that it was written by the same poet who wrote
Sir Gawain and the Green Knight, Patience, and *Purity*, it is noticeable that it is the only one of the hypothetical author's works which

---

[1] *Geoffrey Chaucer* (Oxford, 1934), p. 92.

takes this form. In this case we could not, then, explain away the dream form on the grounds that it was a popular convention. In any case, even if the same poet had written a dozen dream visions (as he may have, for all we know), the popularity of the form is an inadequate explanation for his use of it here; there were other popular forms, and the poet was free to choose the one he preferred for this particular poem.

In the case of Chaucer, it is certainly true that his dream visions are among his more imitative and conventional poems. The interest of most of the scholars who have written about these poems has not gone much beyond tracing sources. Many a critic has regarded them as fairly tiresome exercises of the poet's formative period, and many a commentator seems to turn with relief from this group to the *Troilus* or the *Canterbury Tales*.[2] The *Book of the Duchess* in particular has left many an otherwise enthusiastic Chaucerian cold.[3] It is, however, the consensus that Chaucer's dream poems were an enormous improvement over the earlier and contemporary poems that served him as models. In particular, Chaucerian scholars have noted a specifically dreamlike quality in some of Chaucer's visions. As G. L. Kittredge remarked of the *Book of the Duchess,* Chaucer tried to make his dreams really dreamlike.[4] Lowes noted signs of dream psychology in other Chaucerian dream poems;[5] more recently, Bertrand H. Bronson, among others, has suggested interesting psychological possibilities in Chaucer's visions.[6]

It is notable that almost all the critics who comment on the dreamlike qualities of Chaucer's visions – and also, for that matter, those who doubt the presence or significance of such qualities – assume that this was unusual, and that there was nothing particularly dreamlike about

---

[2] See, e.g., Percy Van Dyke Shelly, *The Living Chaucer* (Philadelphia, 1940), pp. 44-45; Walter Clyde Curry, *Chaucer and the Medieval Sciences* (New York, 1926), p. 233; and Howard Rollin Patch, *On Rereading Chaucer* (Cambridge, Mass., 1948), p. 238.

[3] See, e.g., C. S. Lewis, *The Allegory of Love* (London, 1948), p. 170, and Robert Kilburn Root, *The Poetry of Chaucer* (New York, 1950), pp. 60-63.

[4] *Chaucer and His Poetry* (Cambridge, Mass., 1924), p. 68. For a dissenting view, see Morton W. Bloomfield, *Piers Plowman as a Fourteenth-century Apocalypse* (New Brunswick, N.J., 1962), p. 12; cf. below, p. 103, n. 1.

[5] E.g., *Geoffrey Chaucer*, p. 112.

[6] "The *Book of the Duchess* Reopened", *PMLA*, LXVII (September, 1952), 863-881; also in *Chaucer: Modern Essays in Criticism*, ed. Edward Wagenknecht (New York, 1959), 271-294. – cf. Frederick Tupper, "Chaucer's Lady of the Daisies", *JEGP*, XXI (1922), 293-317.

other medieval dream visions.[7] Yet, certain equally dreamlike qualities have been noted by C. S. Lewis (who does not seem to feel that there is much evidence that Chaucer used the dream as dream to any great advantage) in some of the French poems which served as Chaucer's models.[8] If there are indeed dreamlike qualities in Chaucer and in his French predecessors, is it not possible that there may be such qualities in other dream vision poems? It seems to me that this is not only possible, but a highly significant aspect of the form, and a factor in its enormous popularity.

To what degree, and in what respects, and to what purpose, the Middle English dream visions were like real dreams, is the basic concern of this book. To this end, I shall examine together a group of poems which are not usually considered to be a group, and which may seem to be rather strange bedfellows. *Piers Plowman* and *Pearl*, radically different in many ways from Chaucer's four dream visions, must in this one respect be lumped together with them: they are dream visions. These six great Middle English poems are all, purportedly, dreams. The dream as framework is used very differently by the different poets; the dream may be an excuse for the inclusion of didactic material, or for cutting short an episode. But it also seems frequently to be used as a unifying device, tying together seemingly unrelated material by means of the sort of association and transformation typical of dreams, and, insofar as this is true, the poets must have been making use of what we know as dream psychology. This does not, of course, mean that we can expect in the other dream visions exactly the same sort of use of the dream that Chaucerian scholars have noted in Chaucer's work, but it does seem to raise a question: is it possible that we have been underrating or misinterpreting Middle English dream visions through missing the significance of the fact that they are dreams? For example, did the author of *Piers Plowman* make any use of the fact that his poem purported to be a series of dreams, in a sense analogous to Chaucer's use of the dream convention in the *Book of the Duchess*? Was the dream, to Langland, just a handy excuse for letting his imagination range over a greater territory than real, waking life would permit, or did he make poetic use of dream psychology?

Of course, in using the term "dream psychology" in connection with

---

[7] See, e.g., F. N. Robinson's introduction to the *Book of the Duchess* in his edition of Chaucer's *Works*, 2nd ed. (Cambridge, Mass., 1957), p. 267, and Charles Muscatine, *Chaucer and the French Tradition* (Berkeley, 1957), p. 102.
[8] Cf. below, p. 18.

fourteenth century poets, I do not mean to imply a full-blown post-Freudian system of dream interpretation, but, simply, those facts about the way dreams work which are readily observable by any human being who takes an interest in the matter. The main reason why modern analyses of dream psychology are convincing is the plain fact that they are in accordance with what we all know from our own experience, if we have given that experience any thought. Freud remarked that the peculiarities of the dreaming state are to be found in almost all dream poetry, stating: "Most of the artificial dreams contrived by poets are intended for some such symbolic interpretation, for they reproduce the thought conceived by the poet in a guise not unlike the disguise which we are wont to find in our dreams." [9]

As Freud also noted (p. 184), the basic theories behind many of the ideas on dream interpretation we consider "modern" were quite familiar in the Middle Ages, and are no fresh invention of the twentieth century. Since it is true that medieval theories on the nature of dreams were not so very different from our own, we should not dismiss it as simple coincidence when we find resemblances in Middle English dream poetry to what we can understand as the actual dreaming state. It is true that most of the following arguments for the presence of elements of dream psychology in Middle English poetry rest on an accumulation of seemingly unrelated details, any one of which could admit of a totally different interpretation. In fact, most of these phenomena have been given various explanations, many of which are undoubtedly – although not exclusively – true. The virtue of my interpretation is that it provides one logical explanation for all of these varied phenomena. In many cases, the alternative to accepting a dreamlike phenomena as dreamlike is to find it the result of lack of poetic skill or of muddy thinking; and this conclusion would hardly seem to be giving the hapless but otherwise demonstrably skillful poets the benefit of the doubt.

As a basis for my discussion, it is necessary, first, to look at the dream vision form as it was known to, and developed by, the fourteenth century poets. Then, in order to see how the poets may have tried to make their poetry dreamlike, we must note what a dream was to a fourteenth century poet. Writers of the Middle Ages asserted that dreams were sometimes divine revelations, but they also developed detailed theories of the physical or psychological origins of dreams. It

---

[9] Sigmund Freud, *The Interpretation of Dreams*, in *Basic Writings*, trans. A. A. Brill (New York, 1938), p. 189.

is my thesis that Middle English poets of the fourteenth century show an evident interest in dreams, and exploit, for poetic purposes, a number of aspects of dream psychology and philosophy in their dream visions. I hope to convince the reader that, while these uses vary widely, what contemporary psychology calls "dream-work" is typical of these poems: blending, fusion, and double-meaning are observable in most of them. Multifold and shifting meanings, characteristics of dreams, are also characteristics of these literary works, and a significant earmark of the form in this period.

Medieval allegory and symbolism are usually slippery and shifting, as is a dream; this is particularly true of the allegory and symbolism of the dream visions. My observations indicate that an important reason for the popularity of dream visions is that they are thus a most appropriate vehicle for the type of allegory used in the period; and they have as well a real validity as artistic representations of dream experience.

I

THE DREAM VISION FORM

The medieval dream vision was a literary form used for a great variety of purposes. Many serious and learned works were cast in this form; in Chaucer's century Oresme, writing on astrology, a highly serious matter to men of the fourteenth century, presented a discussion on the movement of the heavens in the form of a dream, containing an allegorical debate between Geometry and Arithmetic.[1] In English poetry of the fourteenth and earlier centuries the dream vision was commonly used for religious themes, as it is in *Piers Plowman* and *Pearl*. Other English poems, although not "dream visions" in form, were said by the poets to have been inspired by a dream, or written in a dream, as, for example, the well-known hymn of Cædmon. The dream as a poetic inspiration has had, of course, a long and honorable history, from classical literature on.[2] As witness to its persistence into more recent times, one need only cite the case of Coleridge and *Kubla Khan*.[3]

1

But when students of medieval poetry speak of the dream vision form as a form they generally are referring to a specific type of dream vision. This form, the tradition which Chaucer knew and used, was primarily, if not exclusively, a vehicle for love poetry. It was, by the fourteenth

---

[1] *De commensurabilitate motuum celestium*, part 3 (ca. 1370). Lynn Thorndike, *A History of Magic and Experimental Science* (New York, 1929-1934), III, 405.
[2] John Barker Stearns (*Studies of the Dream as a Technical Device in Latin Epic and Drama* [Lancaster, Penna., 1927]), discusses many instances in classical poetry, both Greek and Roman, of the dream as an inspiration or as a literary form. Cf. also William Allen Neilson, *The Origins and Sources of the "Court of Love"* (Boston, 1899), pp. 8-10. For the allegory that is such an important element of the medieval dream vision, Neilson remarks on another source, the Bible. Personification is frequently used in the Bible; the Wisdom passages are a notable case. (See Nielson, p. 17 ff.)
[3] Stearns notes the traditions that DeQuincey, Milton (*Para. Lost*, IX. 23), Pope (*Temple of Fame*), Hebbel, and Voltaire were all also among the poets "influenced" by dreams; p. 10.

century, a specific, conventionalized form, the subject matter of which was always love, and, since it was a courtly form the "love" it dealt with was, naturally, "courtly" love.

Of the dozens of poems written in this tradition, one stands out as a sort of prototype: the thirteenth century *Romance of the Rose,* which contains almost all of the elements characteristic of this school of poetry. It was also the best known and most influential example, serving as a model to several generations of court poets,[4] including Geoffrey Chaucer. Aside from his translation of the *Romance* into English, Chaucer turned again and again to it as a "source" for his poetry, and it is therefore a particularly appropriate example of the genre for students of Middle English.

But the *Romance of the Rose* is more than a courtly love vision. Considered as a whole, it is a staggering compendium of medieval thought and interests, of significance for all students of the history, literature, and philosophy of the Middle Ages. However, in examining it specifically as an example of the dream vision, we find that the greater part of the work, the continuation by Jean de Meun, is not as important as the earlier portion written by Guillaume de Lorris. While it is not to be expected that any one poem will contain every single characteristic feature of the dream vision type, this earlier portion comes so close that a discussion of it will serve to describe the entire genre. It is my intention merely to list the elements of this well-known poem which became typical of the dream vision form. If such a listing turns out to be nearly equivalent to a full summary, it is because almost every element of the poem is indeed typical of the form.

First, the poem opens with a brief discussion of dreams and their meaning, or lack of it, making reference to Macrobius' commentary on the *Somnium Scipionis* of Cicero.[5] The poem that follows is, the poet tells us, what he saw in a dream. This element is so typical as to be essential: it gives this type of poetry its name. The poet tells us that he was twenty years old when he had this dream and, of course, in love. Since "courtly love" was thought of as strictly for the young and

---

[4] This is not to be taken as implying that the earmarks of the genre were original with the *Romance of the Rose.* Langlois (*Origines et Sources du Roman de la Rose* [Paris, 1890]) and Neilson (op. cit.) have shown that almost all of the features found in the *Romance* appeared first in earlier courtly poetry not cast in the dream form.

[5] The book is *not* used as motivation for the dream, as Chaucer later used the same book in his *Parliament of Fowls.* The idea of using a book as motivation did become a common feature of such poems later, however, and perhaps this passage contains the germ of the idea; – cf. p. 79.

comely, the poet would have had to be a young man in order to be a lover.

In his dream, the poet awoke and found that it was a beautiful May morning. As numerous commentators have noted, it is not surprising that spring was considered the proper time of year to be associated with youth and love; it still is.[6] This May morning is described at length, with particular reference to flowers and birds. Birds and flowers play many roles in dream vision poetry, ranging from the purely decorative, as here, to a variety of symbolic functions in the story – for example, the Rose itself, which is the poet's lady, or her love.[7]

The poet then found a particularly clear stream and followed it through a meadow to a walled garden. The water motif, rich in connotations to the student of folklore,[8] appears again later in the poem when the poet encounters the well of Narcissus.[9]

The wall surrounding the garden itself is painted with many figures that depict those permanently barred from the garden, among them "Elde" and "Povert".[10] Although it may seem surprising to modern readers, the dreaming poet was evidently not afflicted with "Povert", for he was admitted at once to the garden by the portress, Idleness, a highly appropriate portress for a garden devoted to the time-consuming rites of courtly love.[11]

[6]   Dream visions of this type usually but not invariably set the time as May or April. Some later poems depart from this tradition: the poems that celebrated St. Valentine's Day, for example, would have to take place in February. Among the poems which take place in April rather than May are Machaut's *Dit dou Vergier* and *Dit dou Lyon*. Dream poems in English that do not take place in spring include Chaucer's *House of Fame*, which takes place in December; *Pearl*, which opens in August; and, in the fifteenth century, Skelton's dream visions, *Bouge of Court* and *Garland of Laurel*, both of which take place in fall.

[7]   In other dream visions birds were frequently "characters" in the action, as, for example, in *Melior et Idoine* (an unedited twelfth-century poem) birds serve as judges to the debate, joining in with such partisan enthusiasm that they become combatants themselves. – See Langlois, *Origines*, p. 14.

[8]   See Howard R. Patch, *The Other World According to Descriptions in Medieval Literature* (Cambridge, Mass., 1950), passim; cf. the island in Machaut's *Dit dou Lyon*.

[9]   An interesting descendant of this well appears in Machaut's *Dit de la Fonteine Amoureuse*, where there is a crystal fountain with reliefs showing the stories of Narcissus and the rape of Helen.

[10]   Cf. the wall in the O.F. *Hueline et Aiglantine*, "which no snow or rain or fire can pass"; the wall that excludes the "vilain" in *Li Fablel dou Dieu d'Amours*; and the palace in the O.F. *Florance et Blanchefleur* (Neilson, pp. 36-37, 41).

[11]   Robinson remarks that the "guide" is often a "helpful animal" (p. 266). Machaut's *Dit dou Lyon* is an example. Another interesting variation occurs in

Like Idleness, the other inhabitants of the garden turn out to be personifications. The garden itself belongs to Mirth, and the God of Love holds court there among a throng of allegorical courtiers – Courtesy, Gladness, Beauty, Youth, and "Richesse" are among them. The God of Love himself is, of course, more a personification than a classical deity.[12] A Christian poet of the Middle Ages naturally could not portray him as a true god. But it is interesting that this god, or Venus (who, here as elsewhere, is differentiated from the God of Love and made to represent purely sensual love, as opposed to the elaborate code of courtly love administered by the God of Love) is often worshipped with a sort of parody of Christian ritual.[13] This detail is, however, not noticeable in the *Romance of the Rose*; here, the God of Love is pictured as a feudal lord.

The ever-present birds and flowers appear again in the form of embroidery on the clothing of the God of Love, who also arrives accompanied by birds. In the description of this god Guillaume includes a lengthy passage about his arrows, which were of two types, black and gold, carried for him by his companion, Sweet-Looking.[14]

After his introduction to this group, the poet wanders off and finds the Well of Narcissus and the nearby rose garden. The God of Love follows with his arrows, shoots the poet through the eyes, and thus inspires him with love for the rose he has been admiring. The poet swears fealty to the god, who proceeds to tell him the rules by which he must, as a faithful servant of Love, conduct himself in the future. Among other instructions, he is told to make "songs and complaints" (i.e., love poems) for his lady.[15]

The attempt of the lover to approach the rose follows, with the resulting banishment of Fair-Welcome to the beleaguered fortress.

---

the O.F. *Florance et Blanchefleur* (Neilson, pp. 36-37), where the birds act as guides.

[12] In some medieval poems he is pictured as the lover of Venus rather than as the son; in no case does he bear much resemblance to a classical Cupid.

[13] See, e.g., the twelfth century *Concile de Remiremont*, where a group of nuns conduct a service with Ovid as gospel (Neilson, pp. 31-34; C. S. Lewis, *The Allegory of Love* [London, 1948], pp. 18-20; and Langlois, *Origines*, pp. 6-9), and *La Messe des Oisiaus et li Plais des Chanonesses et des Grises Nonains* by Jean de Conde (fl. 1280-1345) (Neilson, pp. 67-69); cf. Chaucer's *Legend of Good Women*.

[14] Similar arrows of gold, steel, and lead were carried for a similar God of Love by his squire in an early (ca. 1200) Provençal poem by Piere Guilhem (Neilson, p. 24).

[15] Neilson points out (p. 145) that the writing of poetry is often an order of the God of Love, such writing being a penance or expiation.

Here the portion of the poem written by Guillaume ends, but the continuation by Jean de Meun, although it consists largely of the long dissertations on various subjects that most critics term digressions,[16] carries on the story of the lover and the rose, with an account of the siege of the fortress.[17]

These, then, are the characteristic elements of the love vision, the school of poetry to which Chaucer's dream visions belong. There does not appear to be anything strikingly dreamlike about all this. Human beings do not commonly dream in allegorical form – or, at least, in this kind of allegorical form. The dream setting is, rather, used as a setting where the unreal and the imaginative, because they are possible, cannot be judged by the standards of waking reality. It is a device to lend credence to the marvellous; as Langlois remarked, "les songes et les visions offrent un cadre très commode pour exposer des choses que les sens de l'homme à l'état normal ne peuvent percevoir, et qui ont besoin, pour être crues, que leur connaissance s'explique par une seconde vue".[18] The form, as typified by the *Romance of the Rose*, is, however, very much a vision: the imagery and description of the poem are richly visual, and the poem is to a very large extent an account of what the poet *sees* rather than of what he hears or thinks.[19] To this extent perhaps it can be considered dreamlike, for dreams do tend to be largely visual.[20] There may be, however, hints of a closer sort of observation of the traits of the dream in this poem: C. S. Lewis points out (p. 129) that the passage where the lover reaches for the rose and is struck by an arrow has a real resemblance to familiar dream experience: "It is here, for once, that the dream-allegory has something of the flavour of real dreaming. *In mediis conatibus aegri succidimus*! The dreamer can neither reach the Rose nor yet be stayed from approaching it by the five arrows which strike him in succession." Thus, on the whole Gunn's summary of the dream qualities of the *Romance of the Rose* (p. 110, n.) would seem to be a fair one: "Guillaume de Lorris does not attempt to reproduce the phantasmagoric effect of an

[16]   But see Alan M. F. Gunn, *The Mirror of Love* (Lubbock, Texas, 1952).
[17]   Cf. Thibaut's *Roman de la Poire*, which was written at about the same time (Neilson, pp. 56-59).
[18]   *Origines*, p. 55. – This, of course, raises the question of the divine sanction of dreams, a question which will be taken up in Chapter 2.
[19]   This is not, of course, as true for Jean de Meun's portion of the poem, where everyone talks at great length, and there is little description of the appearance of things.
[20]   Cf. Sigmund Freud, *The Interpretation of Dreams*, in *Basic Works*, trans. A. A. Brill (New York, 1938), pp. 361, 487. Cf. also Gunn, pp. 108-109.

actual dream. He seeks rather to achieve a structure logically as well as emotionally and psychologically coherent. Yet there is in his work a sufficient suggestion of dream atmosphere and movement to give it plausibility as a dream."

The French poets who wrote in this genre between the time of Guillaume de Lorris and that of Chaucer added little to the tradition. Those elements they introduce which are not to be found in the *Romance of the Rose* are, generally speaking, derived from other, earlier examples of the poetry of courtly love.[21] But it is perhaps notable that at least one of the French poets known to have been a considerable influence upon Chaucer, Machaut, did to some extent reinforce the dreamlike quality of his vision poems. In this connection, Lewis draws attention particularly to *Dit dou Vergier*, 1199 ff., and *Dit dou Lyon*, 279 ff. The latter passage, which details the poet's meeting with the surprisingly tame lion, may not strike every reader as noticeably dreamlike,[22] but the waking scene in *Dit dou Vergier* is indeed true to everyone's experience.[23]

It would be quite unnecessary to outline here the evidence that Chaucer was much influenced by Guillaume de Lorris and his French successors; these influences have long been a commonplace of Chaucerian scholarship.[24] We find in Chaucer's dream poems – the *Book of the Duchess*, the *House of Fame*, the *Parliament of Fowls*, and the Prologue to the *Legend of Good Women* – most, if not all, of the familiar elements. The May morning, the garden, the God of Love, the birds, even the paintings on walls, are used by Chaucer in one or more of these poems, in all of which love is the subject – or, at least, the ostensible subject. Many of these elements, or very similar features,

---

[21]   As, for example, the singing of the mass by the nightingales in Jean de Condé's *La Messe des Oisiaus et li Plais des Chanonesses et des Grises Nonains*. This is reminiscent of the Ovidian mass of the *Concile de Remiremont*.

[22]   Nothing in Machaut appears to have struck John Livingston Lowes as particularly dreamlike; commenting on *La Fonteinne Amoureuse*, he remarked: "The dream, it is clear, which to Guillaume de Lorris was the heart of his poem, has become to Machaut little more than a clever device to bring an unwontedly lively tale to its climax." – *Geoffrey Chaucer* (Oxford, 1934), p. 72.

[23]   This is not to say, however, that Machaut was the first poet to include a realistic waking scene in a dream poem. The dreaming poet of *Li Fablel dou Dieu d'Amours*, a poem generally considered to be a product of the late thirteenth century, is so delighted at the sight of his beloved that he wakes up; cf. Langlois, *Origines*, p. 17.

[24]   See, e.g., Lisi Cipriani, "Studies in the Influence of the Romance of the Rose Upon Chaucer", *PMLA*, XXII (1907), 552 ff.; Dean Spruill Fansler, *Chaucer and the Roman de la Rose* (New York, 1914); Lowes, op. cit., Ch. III.

also appear in the other fourteenth century dream poems which have
come down to us, but in the case of these other poems there is a significant difference: the subject is not love, or at least not love in the
courtly sense, at all. *Pearl, Piers Plowman, Winner and Waster*, and
the *Parliament of the Three Ages* are all didactic, religious poetry, in
one way or another, and must be considered as to some extent representing a separate tradition.

2

Thus, while scholars generally use the term "dream vision" to refer
to the love vision of the type of the *Romance of the Rose*, the love
vision is only one of the aspects of the dream form in medieval, and
earlier, poetry. The dream as a literary form is, as noted above, not
the creation of the Middle Ages, but a literary tradition going back at
least to classical times. J. B. Stearns has noted many instances in classical poetry. He observes: "In general, the dream fills the role of a
messenger between the divinities or the spirits of the dead and living
mortals. Consequently, the poet, who often regards himself as a priest
of the gods, sometimes receives inspiration by means of dreams, or,
at least, assigns a dream as his reason for composing." [25] The allegorical element in the medieval dream vision is also at least in part a
heritage from classical literature. Ovid and other classical writers were
fond of personification, and the classical gods themselves came to be
regarded as personifications of various human qualities.[26] With these
precedents, and the very significant justification afforded by Biblical
dreams, it does not seem surprising that the dream was considered by
a great many medieval poets to be a highly suitable vehicle for religious
teaching. It was used throughout the Middle Ages for material which
was didactic or supernatural. The dream convention lends a certain
sort of authority, and authority was dear to the medieval public. E. V.
Gordon remarks in his introduction to *Pearl*: "Tales of the past required
their grave authorities, and tales of new things at least an eyewitness,
the author." [27] There are many early examples of religious visions in
English literature, including such works as the Old English *Dream of
the Rood* and the early thirteenth century *Debate Between the Body*

---

[25] *Op. cit.*, pp. ix-x.
[26] Cf. Lewis, Ch. II.
[27] (Oxford, 1953), pp. xiv-xv.

and the Soul, both of which specifically claim to be dreams.[28] All over
Europe didactic poems galore were cast in the dream form,[29] including
the influential *De planctu Naturae* of Alanus de Insulis.

In these poems allegory is at least as prominent as in the "love
vision", but here it is, of course, a Christian theological allegory. The
popularity of the dream as a vehicle for allegory started with its use
for this theological allegory; its carry-over into courtly love poetry
is, as Langlois remarks, another of the many instances of the courtly
poets' borrowings from specifically Christian literature: "J'ai montré
déjà comment les poètes érotiques se sont approprié, pour l'enseigne-
ment de leur religion, certains procédés de la littérature chrétienne; c'est
un emprunt nouveau que, sciemment ou non, ils on fait à la même
litterature, lorsqu'ils ont adopté le songe comme moyen de commu-
niquer avec leur divinité." [30]

The love vision, then, was descended mainly from courtly poetry in
forms other than the dream, and apparently borrowed the dream idea
from serious religious poetry, just as it borrowed other elements of
Christian theory, worship, and practice in the service of a "God of
Love" somewhat modelled on the Christian God. But in its turn the
love vision was eventually drawn upon by religious poets, and thus we
find that the serious didactic poems of the fourteenth century in England, if they are dream visions, have many of the same earmarks as
those written more directly under the courtly tradition: *Piers Plowman*
and the *Parliament of the Three Ages* both begin with a May morning;
Pearl and *Winner and Waster* are full of birds; in the latter three poems
the dreaming poet finds himself in a marvelous garden not too unlike
the garden of the Rose; all four describe at some point a stream, such
as the one along which the lover of the *Romance of the Rose* strolled.
Like the *Romance,* all of these are definitely visions in that they have
a wealth of vivid imagery, presenting scene after scene to the eye in
terms of color and visual detail.

Langlois said of the love vision school of poetry, "l'allégorie fait
essentiellement partie du songe; c'est elle qui le distingue des autres
genres de vision".[31] This distinction looks back to such earlier vision

---

[28]   On the *Debate,* see Albert C. Baugh, "The Middle English Period", in *A
Literary History of England,* ed. A. C. Baugh (New York, 1948), pp. 162-164.
It is, as Baugh remarks, related to a number of poems and sermons on the
same subject, the earliest of which is a twelfth century Latin poem.
[29]   For a list of examples, see Langlois, *Origines,* p. 57.
[30]   *Ibid.,* p. 58.
[31]   *Ibid.*

poetry as *De planctu Naturae*; it certainly no longer applies to the Middle English poems just mentioned, since they all have many of the same qualities as the love visions. The question then remains: in what *way* is the allegory part of a dream? Do these poems make use in any way of a recognizable psychology of dreams? And, of course, before we can consider whether the poets deliberately tried to make their dreams "dreamlike", we must consider what they might have understood as dreamlike. Thinkers of the Middle Ages had given a great deal of attention to the origins, nature, and meaning of dreams. In the case of Chaucer, there is a considerable body of evidence that he was familiar, at least in part, with this literature, and that in writing his vision poetry he was not only following a specific poetic tradition but also supplementing it with recollections from his reading in scientific and theological literature. It is to this literature that we must look first for an understanding of what a "dream" may have meant to a fourteenth century poet.

II

MEDIEVAL DREAM INTERPRETATION

What was a dream like to a fourteenth century poet? With all due allowance for the poet's own observation and insight, we must be careful not to look for ideas which such a poet could not possibly have known. It seems necessary first to try to establish what was generally thought by men of the time, particularly by authors with whom our poets may have been familiar. All of this medieval opinion appears to fall into one of three patterns: first, that dreams are divinely (or diabolically) caused, and therefore may show the future or impart knowledge in a supernatural way; second, that dreams have purely physical or psychological causes; or, third, that some dreams have supernatural causes, while others have purely physical causes.

To a certain extent, belief in the divine origin of dreams was a religious necessity. To contradict its possibility would have been to contradict the authority of the Bible. However, because dream interpretation was also intimately connected with astrology and other forms of augury, it was therefore partially suspect.[1] This double-horned view led to an extremely complicated and touchy theological question, which necessitated classifying dreams as to type, so that a way could be found to tell which dreams were of divine origin and therefore legitimate.[2]

[1] Lynn Thorndike (*A History of Magic and Experimental Science* [New York, 1929-1934], II, 319) points out that Michael Scot, a thirteenth century astrologer, believed the interpretation of dreams (along with other methods of augury) to be true, but "forbidden as infamous and evil". Nevertheless, he included in his book an "exposition of dreams for each day of the moon". – c.f. Theodore Otto Wedel (*The Medieval Attitude Toward Astrology, Particularly in England* [New Haven, 1920], p. 117): "The early church had made no distinction between a true and a false astrology. The Church of the thirteenth century, by making just this distinction, was enabled to entertain an enthusiasm for the moderate science of Ptolemy, and to preserve, at the same time, pious scorn for astrological magic."
[2] One of the earliest of these attempts to divide dreams into separate categories was that of Philo Judaeus in the first century. His theory did not differentiate between divine and diabolical dreams, as most later theories did, but distinguished between clearly prophetic dreams, needing no interpretation; medium-clear

Since earliest times men had believed that dreams may foretell future events.[3] For medieval Christians, always believers in "authority", this tradition was reinforced by the authority not only of the Bible but also of classical writers, such as Plutarch and Pliny;[4] Christian authorities included St. Augustine (354-430),[5] St. Hildegarde of Bingen (1098-1179),[6] Adelard of Bath (fl. 1130),[7] and St. Thomas Aquinas (1225 or 1227-1272);[8] and a number of widely known "dream books", some of which were attributed to such biblical prophets as Joseph and Daniel.[9] Some ideas common in medieval dream books were that the meaning of the same dream would vary depending on whether it appeared to a king (or other man of high rank) or a commoner; that dreams were more likely to be significant if they occurred at certain times of the night, seasons of the year, or phases of the moon and stars; that "true" dreams were sent by God and "false" dreams by the devil; that certain individuals − magicians − had the power of sending dreams to others; that certain gems or herbs would bring true dreams or ward off false dreams; and that certain places were especially propitious for dreaming true dreams.[10]

---

dreams of a more or less allegorical nature; and confused prophetic dreams that require careful interpretation. − Thorndike, I, 358.

[3] Even today this belief is by no means dead; a recent article in a popular national weekly magazine (Gardner Murphy, "The Truth About Clairvoyance", *This Week*, February 24, 1957, pp. 16-17) cites, in a thoroughly sober manner and in a context purporting to be a scientific investigation, several examples of dreams that "came true." For that matter, many modern psychologists of unquestionable legitimacy make allowances for the possibility of some sort of telepathy; cf. below, p. 52.

[4] Cf. Thorndike, I, 205: "The extent of Plutarch's faith in dreams may be inferred from his discussion of the problem, why are dreams in autumn the least reliable?" (*Symposium*, VIII, 10) − Pliny discussed dreams that had revealed various truths in *Nat. hist.* xxv, 6 (ca. 77 A.D.); Thorndike, I, 56.

[5] *The City of God*, trans. Marcus Dods (New York, 1950), X, ll, p. 315; cf. also *De spiritu et anima*, cap. xxv, and *Liber de divinatione daemonum*, cap. v; Thorndike, I, 509; Walter Clyde Curry, *Chaucer and the Medieval Sciences* (New York, 1926), p. 210.

[6] *Hildegardis causae et curae*, ed. Paulus Kaiser (Leipsig, 1903), 82-83; Thorndike, II, 154.

[7] *De eodem et diverso*, ed. H. Willner (Münster, 1903), p. 13; Thorndike, II, 40.

[8] *Summa*, II, ii, 95, art. 6; Thorndike, II, 605.

[9] Others were attributed to various Greek authors, such as Dionysius of Rhodes. The most influential single work of this group was the 'ονειροκρίτικα of Artemidorus (2nd century A.D.), a lengthy compilation of interpretations of specific dreams, conditions that must be met if the interpretation is to be valid, and so forth. See Thorndike, II, 290-297, and Werner Wolff, *The Dream − Mirror of Conscience* (New York, 1952), pp. 20-23.

[10] Thorndike, I, 56, 205, 284.

The idea that dreams foretell the future did not go unchallenged, however, either in classical times or in the Middle Ages. Aristotle completely discounted the idea of divine inspiration, explaining dreams as caused solely by physical or psychological causes; he explained that dreams which appear to "come true" are either mere coincidence or explained by the fact that dreams may be themselves the causes of thought or action.[11] J. B. Stearns remarks:

Apparently Greek speculation as early at least as Plato reached the conclusion that the reliability of the dream as a means of divination depended upon the state of the physical organism during sleep; when the body is clogged with food and drink in excess, phantasmagorical dreams result, but temperance produces clear and divine dreams. This doctrine gave rise to the Pythagorean prohibition of the bean as an article of diet (cf. e.g. Cicero De div. i, 62; ii. 119; Pliny, Hist. nat. xviii 12 ...) [12]

Here is the germ of the second important school of thought in the Middle Ages: that dreams result from natural, physical causes, such as the state of health of the dreamer, or that they are of psychological origin and mirror our waking thoughts.[13]

Some Christians accepted the "natural" interpretation of dreams to the complete exclusion of any supernatural aspects. St. Basil (ca. 329-379) lumped the interpretation of dreams with "old wives' tales" as completely preposterous,[14] and Rufinus, in debunking astrology, compares "successful" explanation to "dreams of which men can make nothing at the time, but 'when any event occurs, then they adapt what they saw in the dream to what has occurred' ".[15] The Middle English

---

[11] "On Sleep" and "On Prophecy", in Basic Writings, trans. J. J. Beare (New York, 1941); n.b. pp. 375-377, 381. Cf. Wolff, pp. 17-18.

[12] John Barker Stearns, Studies of the Dream as a Technical Device in Latin Epic and Drama (Lancaster, Penna., 1927), p. 68. – Cicero goes to the length of completely denying the possibility of divine inspiration in dreams; see "On Divination", in Treatises, trans. I. D. Yonge (London, 1871); cf. Wolff, p. 19.

[13] Stearns has also found a number of examples of the theory of psychological causes in classical Latin poetry (p. 47): "In one sense most of the dreams portrayed in Latin epic and drama are natural dreams: that is, the typical dream-episode is connected in subject matter with the daily preoccupations and pursuits of the dreamer. For instance, the dreams of Aeneas in most cases reflect the anxieties of his mind during his waking hours. Certainly the dreams of Dido reveal the lovesick woman's cares in a graphic manner." – Lucretius had some very interesting theories on the psychological meaning of dreams, considering them to come from the unconscious mind, reflecting wish-fulfillment and conscience; see De rerum natura, Bk. IV, trans. William E. Leonard (New York, 1916), p. 173; cf. Wolff, pp. 19-20.

[14] Hexaemeron, III, 9; Thorndike, I, 487.

[15] Recognitions, X, 12 (ca. 400); Thorndike, I, 413.

Ancrene Riwle, while it attributes dreams to a supernatural cause, considers them entirely lures of the devil, and therefore of no account: "If you think that you see a vision, whether in a waking state or in a dream, count it no more than a delusion, for it is only his [the devil's] deceit." [16]

The "natural" theory of dreams was remarkably elaborated in medieval medicine, and, as Lowes remarked, "Fourteenth-century medicine, like its twentieth-century descendant, was half psychology, and in its emphasis on dreams as a means of diagnosis anticipated Freud." [17]

If, then, it was recognized that dreams could result from purely natural causes, how could this be reconciled with belief in divine origin, and therefore with the possibility of predicting the future through dreams? Medieval philosophy solved the conflict by classifying dreams into entirely separate, although occasionally overlapping, categories, and thus saw no reason why both theories of the origin of dreams could not be true. This may sound impossible, yet it is not far from current theories on the meaning of dreams, which take physical factors into account as quite separate from the "unconscious" causes of dreams.

One of the earliest exponents of this combined view was Plato, who considered some dreams divine, but others as merely revealing man's desires or reflecting his thought.[18] Galen (131-201) believed that dreams were affected by bodily conditions and by one's daytime life and thought, but also that, at least to some extent, dreams predict the future.[19] Galen also expressed another idea that became an integral part of later dream philosophy: the idea that the healthy, quiet mind can mirror "spirits" in sleep. Thus, an ill or disturbed individual would have dreams that were the result of his illness, his disturbance, or excitement; but a perfectly healthy, calm individual, undisturbed by purely physical factors, could be attuned to spiritual influences and dream "true" dreams.[20]

---

[16]   Trans. M. B. Salu, with introduction by Dom Gerard Sitwell (and Preface by J. R. R. Tolkien) (Notre Dame, Indiana, 1956), p. 100.

[17]   John Livingston Lowes, *Essays in Appreciation* (Boston, 1936), pp. 94-95.

[18]   *Republic*, trans. Benjamin Jowett (New York, 1944), p. 467; *Phaedo,* in *Dialogues,* trans. Jowett (New York, 1892), p. 444; cf. Wolff, p. 16.

[19]   He stated that he took up medicine because of instructions given in a dream. Most interestingly, he also said that dreams often provide a clue to the health or illness of the dreamer and that he often used them as an aid to diagnosis. *Hippocratic Commentaries,* ed. Kuhn (Leipsig, 1821-1833), XVI, 222-223; *De anatom. administ.,* ed. Kuhn, II, 217, 224-225, 660; *Diagnosis From Dreams,* ed. Kuhn, VI, 833; Thorndike, I, 123, 177-178.

[20]   Cf. Curry, pp. 203-206.

Various philosophers devised systems to distinguish between the divinely inspired sheep and the naturally caused goats. At first, the distinction was a simple one, between human and divine causes.[21] The astrologer Haly divided dreams into three, rather than two, classes: the vision sent by God; the dream caused by planetary influences; and the dream proceeding from "humours" of the body. Of these three, the first is bound to be always true, the third always false, the second sometimes true and sometimes false.[22] Another threefold classification was that of Petrus de Abano, who spoke of dreams (*somnia*) as *somnium naturale, somnium animale,* and *somnium coeleste* (or *divinum*).[23] Here the distinction between the *somnium animale* and the *somnium naturale* does not, apparently, have reference to astrology and bodily humours, but to physical vs. psychological causes.

By the fourteenth century the most accepted systems of dream classification had been further refined into five gradations. Two of the most widely known dream commentators of the Middle Ages were John of Salisbury (ca. 1120-1180) and Macrobius (ca. 400), and their systems of dream classification were essentially the same. These classifications were:

1. *insomnium,* nightmare or troubled dream;
2. *visium,* apparition or hallucination;
3. *somnium,* ordinary or enigmatic dream;
4. *oraculum,* oracular or prophetic dream;
5. *visio,* prophetic vision or visionary dream.[24]

Of the first type of dream, John of Salisbury said they are "in general the result of insobriety or drunkenness, different emotions, turmoil of

---

[21] Iamblicus, in *De abstinentia,* III, 2-3 (ca. 300), made just this distinction, but retained the provision that "human" dreams could occasionally be "true". Thorndike, I, 314. Gregory of Nyssa (4th century) made the same distinction, but broke the ordinary, "human" type into two categories, those caused by memory and those influenced by bodily stimuli. See "Gregory of Nyssa", in *The Ante-Nicene Fathers,* vol. II, trans. Peter Holmes (New York, 1918); cf. Wolff, p. 24. As late as the early fourteenth century this basic twofold division was made by Arnoldus of Villa Nova (1235-1315); see *Des weltberühmten und hocherfahrnen philosophi u. medici Arnoldi de Villa Nova chymische schriften...* (Vienna, 1748); Wolff, p. 26.

[22] *De indiciis astrorum,* Pars III, cap. xii; Curry, p. 210.

[23] *Liber Conciliator differentiarum philosophorum precipueque medicorum appelatus,* dif. CLVII, fol. 202 (ca. 1300); Curry, p. 207.

[24] Macrobius, *Commentary on the Dream of Scipio,* trans. William Harris Stahl (New York, 1952), p. 88, and John of Salisbury, *Policraticus,* trans. Joseph B. Pike (Minneapolis, 1938), pp. 75-79.

feeling, or vestiges of thoughts." [25] In this connection, he quoted (p. 82) the words of Cato:

> Regard not dreams; the mind of man awake
> But hopes for his desires, asleep beholds the same.

Macrobius said that such dreams "may be caused by mental or physical distress, or anxiety about the future: the patient experiences in dreams vexations similar to those that disturb him during the day." [26] He felt that this sort of dream, as well as the second type, was "not worth mentioning since they have no prophetic significance". [27]

The second type (*visium*), according to Macrobius (p. 89), coming "upon one in the moment between wakefulness or slumber", includes the incubus, "which, according to popular belief, rushes upon people in sleep and presses them with a weight which they can feel". John of Salisbury also includes the incubus in this category, in which, he says, one sees strange forms, contrary to nature. He felt that such dreams call for the attention of a doctor as symptoms of mental illness. [28]

The ordinary, or enigmatic, dream, according to John of Salisbury, "contains images of events wrapped as it were in a cloak of disguise, and it is with this disguise that the art of interpreting dreams deals. The dream at times pertains to oneself, at times to another person; sometimes it is common to both of these, at others it is of public or general application." [29] Macrobius states similarly that such a dream "conceals with strange shapes and veils with ambiguity the true meaning of the information being offered, and requires an interpretation for its understanding". He goes on (p. 90) to divide this category into five sub-categories:

    (1) personal: "he himself is doing or experiencing";
    (2) alien: someone else is "doing or experiencing";
    (3) social: others and himself are involved;

[25] *Policraticus*, p. 76.
[26] Pp. 88-89. Macrobius gives a number of examples: "mental variety includes ... lover who dreams of possessing his sweetheart or of losing her, or the man who fears the plots or might of an enemy and is confronted with him in his dream or seems to be fleeing him. The physical variety might be illustrated by one who has been suffering from hunger or thirst and dreams that he is raving and searching for food or drink or has found it. Anxiety about the future would cause a man to dream that he is gaining a prominent position or office as he had hoped or that he is being deprived of it as he feared."
[27] *Ibid.*, p. 88.
[28] *Policraticus*, p. 76.
[29] *Ibid.*, pp. 76-77.

(4) public: involving public misfortune or benefit;

(5) universal: "some change has taken place in the sun, moon, planets, sky or regions of the earth".

We are dealing with an oracular dream, according to John of Salisbury (p. 79), "when a communication is made in sleep by the agency of a second person, and this individual is of honorary position, worthy of reference". He quotes Seneca: "an oracle is the pronouncement of divine will by the mouth of man". (In this case, "man" means anything – spirit, for example – that assumes human form.) Macrobius agrees, defining the term further (p. 90) as having meaning when "a parent, or a pious or revered man, or a priest, or even a god clearly reveals what will or will not transpire, and what action to take or to avoid".[30]

In the last type of dream, the vision, "information also is at one time conveyed more explicitly, at another more obscurely; it is revealed now directly to the mind and again by the medium of a third person. But when this knowledge is imparted directly in a flood of light, it becomes a vision by virtue of the fact that it seems to be presented to the eye in complete and concrete form."[31] John of Salisbury cautions, however, that the vision may be clouded by allegory. Macrobius states (p. 90) that one can identify a dream as prophetic "if it actually comes true. For example, a man dreams of the return of a friend who has been staying in a foreign land, thoughts of whom never enter his mind. He goes out and presently meets his friend and embraces him."

Both commentators agree in calling the most common the third type of dream, "which stretches before the body of truth a curtain, as it were, of allegory".[32] Hence, of course, the difficulties of dream interpretation. John of Salisbury appears to have been quite uneasy about dream interpretation. Although he gives it sufficient credence to justify a long passage on the effects of different places and seasons of the year on dreams, saying that interpretation may be by opposites or by likes, he feels on the whole that dream interpretation is beyond human wisdom: dreams are ambiguous, and anyone who confidently states meaning (that is, anyone not divinely guided) is a fool. He is most contemptuous of the popular *Dream-Book of Daniel,* arguing that Joseph and Daniel interpreted by divine inspiration, not by any such "science" of interpretation.[33]

[30] Cf. *Policraticus,* p. 77.
[31] *Policraticus,* p. 78.
[32] *Ibid.,* p. 81.
[33] *Ibid.,* pp. 75-86. – Both Macrobius (p. 92) and John of Salisbury (p. 75)

The difficulties of analyzing this unreliable "ordinary" type of dream were not, however, the only problems besetting the medieval dream interpreter. There was the further possibility of two or more types overlapping. In his analysis of the dream of Scipio, Macrobius states that it "embraces the three reliable types mentioned above, and also has to do with all five varieties of the enigmatic dream".[34] It is interesting to note that Jean de Meun in the *Romance of the Rose* came to an entirely different conclusion about this dream, considering it a dream brought on by meditation and therefore false:

> On qui, par grant devocion,
> En trop grant contemplacioun,
> Font apareir en leur pensees
> Les choses qu'il ont pourpensees,
> E les cuident tout proprement
> Voeir defors apertement.
> E ce n'est fors trufle e mençonge,
> Ainsinc con de l'ome qui songe,
> Qui veit, ce cuide, en leur presences
> Les espituens sustances,
> Si con fist Scipion jadis;
> E veit enfer e paradis,
> E ceil, e air, e mer, e terre,
> E tont quanque l'en i peut querre.[35]

Jean de Meun's ideas on dreams have, of course, a particular interest for the student of Chaucer, since we can be sure that Chaucer read

---

spoke of the idea of the gates of horn and ivory, taken from the *Aeneid*, through which clear, and therefore true, and ambiguous, less true, dreams are spoken of as passing.

[34] Pp. 90-91.

[35] *Le Roman de la Rose*, ed. Ernest Langlois (Paris, 1912), IV, 226, ll. 18357-18370. Ellis (*Romance of the Rose* [London 1960], III, 124-125) translates these lines:

> One will with great
> Devotion muse and meditate,
> Until before his mind is brought
> The objects that his soul hath sought,
> And with eyes he thinks to see
> Things of substantiality,
> Though all is false, and doth but seem,
> In fashion as a man may dream
> That sees he clearly with his eyes
> Objects which are but shadowy lies,
> (Even as Scipio dreamed how heaven
> And hell unto his view were given,
> And sky and earth, end air and sea,
> And all things that therein may be.)

and admired the *Romance of the Rose,* while the other dream authorities he knew remain a matter of some debate.[36]

While the *Romance* begins with a confident assertion,

> That dremes signifiaunce be
> Of good and harm to many wightes,
> That dremen in her slep a-nyghtes
> Ful many thynges covertly,
> That fallen after al openly,[37]

like so many of Guillaume de Lorris' ideas, this is in direct conflict with the view of Jean de Meun, whose long passage on dreams compares them to reflections in distorting mirrors.[38] On the whole, Jean seems to be convinced that most dreams can be traced to our daytime preoccupations. In this connection he includes a passage adapted from Claudian:

> Les uns en chambres soulacier,
> Les autres veit par bois chacier,
> Par montaignes e par rivieres,
> Par prez, par vignes, par faschieres;
> E songe plaiz e juigemenz,
> E guerres e tourneiemenz,
> E baleries e queroles,
> E ot vieles e citoles,
> E flaire espices odoureuses,
> E gouste choses savoureuses,
> E sent entre ses braz s'amie,
> Touteveis n'i est ele mie.[39]

[36] See, e.g., E. P. Anderson, "Some Notes on Chaucer's Treatment of the Somnium Scipionis", *Proced. of the Amer. Philol. Assn.,* XXXIII (1902), p. xcviii; Stahl, Introduction to Macrobius, p, 53; Pauline Aiken, "Vincent of Beauvais and Dame Pertelote's Medicine", *Speculum,* X (1935), 281; A. Hamilton Thompson, "Classical Echoes in Medieval Authors", *History,* XXXIII (1948), p. 37.

[37] *The Romaunt of the Rose,* in *The Works of Geoffrey Chaucer,* ed. F. N. Robinson, 2nd ed. (Cambridge, Mass., 1957), p. 565, ll. 16-20.

[38] Langlois, IV, 224; Ellis, III, 122. – Gunn (*Mirror of Love* [Lubbock, Texas, 1952], p. 270, n.) sees this as fitting his idea that Jean is demonstrating "false generation"; he states that "the consideration of dreams is an expansion of the ideas of false vision presented in an earlier passage on optical science".

[39] Langlois, IV, 226-227, ll. 18377-18388. Cf. Ellis, III, 125:

> While this man loveth chamber play,
> Another to the chase all day
> Betakes him on the mountain wide,
> Or to the woods or river-side:
> One dreams of judgements, suits, and pleas,
> Another of war and skirmishes
> And tournaments, while song and dance
> A third man dreams of, and perchance

This is the same passage from Claudian that Chaucer used in the *Parliament of Fowls*.[40]

Among the other writers on dreams whose works Chaucer may have known, Vincent of Beauvais (fl. 1250) should be mentioned. Although Vincent accepted such commonplaces as the influence of astrology, demons, angelic revelation, and the physical and mental condition of the dreamer,[41] there is one particularly interesting point in his discussion not clearly brought out by other commentators. This is a theological question: if dreams predict the future, is that future then irrevocably destined? How about the doctrine of free will? The whole question of free will vs. predestination, one of the thorniest problems of the theology of the day, is entirely too complicated a question to be handled here in all its ramifications.[42] But dreams, if they predicted the future, were one of the ramifications. Vincent finds in this aspect of dreams an interesting explanation of their ambiguity: if dreams cannot be causes of the future, but simply signs, since the events that they signify do not yet exist, they cannot indicate these non-existent events clearly; they can only suggest them.[43]

Curry points out that among all these commentators there was a general agreement, an acceptance of the division of dreams into the various types already discussed: "Among philosophers, astrologers, medical men, and theologicans there are neither essential differences of opinion nor grounds for controversy. There is only a variety of emphasis . . . I cannot imagine Chaucer's having been ignorant of these

---

> Another solaceth his soul
> With fiddle-bow or sweet citole,
> Eats well and sniffs the savourous air
> Which sweet scent of spices bear,
> And lastly full contentment grasps
> When in his arms his love he clasps.

[40] Lines 99-105. This is a much more literal translation than Jean de Meun's. Cf. Claudian, *Panegyricus de sexto consulatu Honorii Augusti, Praefatio*, in *Works*, with trans. by Maurice Platnauer (New York, 1922), II, 70-73. Robert A. Pratt ("Chaucer's Claudian", *Speculum*, XXII [1947], 419-429) shows that in most medieval manuscripts of *Liber Catonianus*, a popular schoolbook, this preface appeared as preface to Book III of Claudian's *De raptu Proserpinae*, and this is probably where Chaucer found the passage. – As Frederick Tupper remarked ("Chaucer's Lady of the Daisies", *JEGP*, XXI [1922], 297 n.), the passage "suggests the chief Freudian tenet that 'a dream is the imaginary fulfillment of some ungratified wish.' "

[41] *Speculum naturale*, XXVII, 52-61; Thorndike, ll. 467.

[42] Cf. *Romance of the Rose*, trans. Ellis, III, 84-109; Boethius, *The Consolation of Philosophy*, Book IV; St. Augustine, *The City of God*, V, 9-10, pp. 152, 158.

[43] *Speculum naturale*, XXVII, 52-61; Thorndike, II, 467.

universally accepted conclusions."[44] Thus far, Curry is undoubtedly right. But, he continues, Chaucer saw the difficulty: "With the vision of last night upon the table, how is one to know whether it is merely a *somnium naturale*, or a *somnium animale*, or a revelation, or an illusion, or a phantom?" This question would seem to imply that Chaucer accepted the conclusions of the authorities he knew, an assumption that may be unjustified. Does his familiarity with these beliefs necessarily mean that he subscribed to them? Was the question of distinguishing one from the other the only question left unanswered in his mind? It is only fair to look for the answer in Chaucer's own work, to consider what he had to say on the subject. Chaucer and his contemporaries had a very great deal to say on the subject, both directly and by implication – i.e., through the inclusion of dream sequences in their poetry – and a look at their comments on, and descriptions of, dreams may be of great help in deciding what they understood a dream to be.

[44] Pp. 217-218.

III

THE POETS ON THE INTERPRETATION OF DREAMS

Aside from their use as a "form" in poetry, dreams are prominent as a topic, or occurrence, in Middle English poetry. Most of the poets make occasional references to dreams, or include dream sequences in their work. It is, however, not particularly surprising that the poet who wrote the greatest number of dream visions – so far as we know – also had the most to say about dreams *per se*; it would seem appropriate to turn first to this poet, Geoffrey Chaucer, on the subject of dreams.

1

There are many dreams in Chaucer's works, and a number of discussions of dreams, of which the three earliest appear in the *House of Fame,* the *Parliament of Fowls,* and *Troilus and Criseyde.*[1] The first two, occurring in the first person, may be regarded as Chaucer speaking – if we are careful to remember Chaucer's irony.

Beginning the *House of Fame* with the wish that all dreams may "turn to good", he continues:

> For hyt is wonder, be the roode,
> To my wyt, what causeth swevenes
> Eyther on morwes or on evenes;
> And why th'effect folweth of somme,
> And of somme hit shal never come;
> Why that is an avisioun
> And this a revelacioun,
> Why this a drem, why that a sweven,
> And noght to every man lyche even.[2]

[1] While the dreamer in the *Book of the Duchess* does comment that his dream was "So wonderful, that never yit/ Y trowe no man had the wyt/ To konne wel my sweven rede" (ll. 277-279), there is no general discussion of dreams in this poem, and it is therefore omitted from consideration in this particular chapter. It is discussed below in Chapter 5.

[2] Lines 2-10. All citations from Chaucer in my text are from the *Works,* ed. F. N. Robinson, 2nd ed. (Cambridge, Mass., 1957). – J. A. W. Bennett (*The*

After a few more lines on the complications of dream interpretation, he concludes that he just can't bother his poor brain with all of this. This is either heresy against the accepted authorities on dreams or a comic assumption of innocent stupidity, and probably it is a compound of the two. Kemp Malone remarks that "all this was meant to be funny. Chaucer's audience knew perfectly well that he was a man of learning and anything but a lazybones." [3] While this is undoubtedly true, the passage does convey a suggestion of the writer's true attitude; perhaps one might say that this is an attitude of scepticism, since it questions "universally accepted conclusions". [4] The lines that follow give in detail the possible causes of dreams, all of them familiar: "complexions" (i.e., "humours"); weakness of the brain caused by abstinence, sickness, for example; long contemplation or study before bedtime; lovers' desires and worries; spirits; and the possible prophetic abilities of the soul: "But why the cause is, noght wot I." [5] Here we have a statement implying that the author is thinking in terms of *a* cause for dreams – not many causes, nor of the problem as a decision among them in interpreting a particular dream; he is questioning the various theories of causes. His conclusion, even if a comic one, is simply that he cannot understand it all.

The passage on dreams in the *Parliament of Fowls* (11. 99-108) is, as already indicated, a very close translation of Claudian. It expresses the idea that we dream of our waking preoccupations:

> The wery huntere slepynge in his bed,
> To wode ayeyn his mynde goth anon;
> The juge dremeth how his plees been sped;
> The cartere dremeth how his cartes gon;
> The riche, of gold; the knyght fyght with his fon;
> The syke met he drynketh of the tonne;
> The lovere met he hath his lady wonne.
>
> Can I not seyn if that the cause were
> For I hadde red of Affrican byforn,
> That made me to mete that he stod there . . .

Parlement of Foules: An Interpretation [Oxford, 1957], p. 53) seems to suggest that "sweven" is exactly equivalent to *somnium* – i.e., as a *kind* of dream. This distinction seems dubious, in view of the fact that the various words for dreams in Middle English were frequently used interchangeably. The *Pearl*-poet calls his dream a "drem" in l. 1170 and a "sweuen" in l. 62, as well as an "avysyoun" in l. 1184.

[3]   *Chapters on Chaucer* (Baltimore, 1951), p. 48.
[4]   Walter Clyde Curry, *Chaucer and the Medieval Sciences* (New York, 1926), p. 218; cf. above, p. 32.
[5]   Line 52.

Again, Chaucer will not say what caused his dream. But he does not here emphasize his "ignorance", and the whole context suggests strongly that he did dream of Scipio because he had just been reading of him.

The opinions expressed on dreams in *Troilus and Criseyde* are those of Chaucer's characters, not necessarily those of the poet.[6] Naturally, what Pandarus and Troilus have to say on the subject of dreams is in each case appropriate to the character. Troilus, the believer in predestination, believes his dreams to be prophetic. Pandarus first scoffs at dreams entirely, but then says that they are very difficult to interpret correctly – administering not very effective consolation. Perhaps the difference in Pandarus' attitude arises from the difference between the two occasions on which Troilus reports his dreams.

In the first case, Troilus has suffered from a series of frightening dreams: that he was alone in a horrible place, that he had fallen into the hands of his enemies, and that he was falling from a high place. Tatlock remarks that "dreams of falling are characteristic of anxiety neurosis, assuredly Troilus' case".[7] Although this observation is based on knowledge probably not current in the fourteenth century, there is always the possibility that Chaucer may have observed it himself. At any rate, it agrees with medieval theories on dreams, since this sort of dream would be expected in the case of a person whose mind was disturbed. Medieval medicine might classify this series of dreams as phantasma, caused by a superfluity of melancholy.[8] Pandarus, on hearing of the dreams, says just this: that these dreams are obviously caused by melancholy.

This is exactly what Boccaccio's Pandaro had said.[9] But Chaucer's Pandarus goes on to say that he wouldn't give a straw for the significance of any dream; no man knows what they mean. His reason, interestingly, is that the explanations of dreams are too many and too

[6] Many readers have a tendency to say, "Chaucer says" or "Shakespeare says" – when they mean, "Pandarus says", or "Mercutio says". It must be clear that in the *Troilus*, Chaucer, in his own person, has nothing at all to say on dreams. Considering the fact that he has much to say on other subjects and that he was obviously deliberate in his refusals to commit himself in his earlier discussions of the subject, this is, perhaps, significant in itself.
[7] J. S. P. Tatlock, "The People in Chaucer's *Troilus*", *PMLA*, LVI (1941), p. 103, n.; also in *Chaucer: Modern Essays in Criticism*, ed. Edward Wagenknecht (New York, 1959), pp. 328-347, but this note is omitted.
[8] Cf. Curry, pp. 208-209.
[9] *Filostrato* V, 32; Robert K. Gordon, trans., *The Story of Troilus as Told by Benoit de Sainte-Maure, Giovanni Boccaccio, Geoffrey Chaucer and Robert Henryson* (London, 1934), p. 96.

inconclusive. This idea is reminiscent of Chaucer's confusion in the *House of Fame*: again, it is a listing of all the things said to cause dreams; an avowal of the futility of trying to make sense of it all.[10]

But the second time Troilus reports a dream, the case is somewhat different. He has been just as melancholy, his mind even more troubled; but the dream itself is not of the wild, nightmarish type, but of a figurative nature. He sees Criseyde kissing a boar. He accepts this dream at once as being allegorical, signifying Criseyde's unfaithfulness, although he does not know whom the boar may signify.[11] Pandarus reacts in these words:

> Have I nat seyde er this,
> That dremes many a maner man bygile?
> And whi? For folk expounden hem amys.
> How darstow seyn that fals thy lady ys,
> For any drem, right for thyn owene drede?
> Lat be this thought; thow kanst no dremes rede.[12]

This could be just another way of saying that there are too many theories about the causes of dreams and that there is no use trying to determine the correct one. But he goes on to suggest that the boar in the dream may be Criseyde's father; therefore he has obviously abandoned his former view that dreams cannot be interpreted and is simply trying to find a different interpretation. Chaucer gives no explanation for this change in Pandarus' attitude, but it is quite possible that he meant us to understand that Pandarus knew that Troilus' interpretation was probably correct (there is no reason why he may not have known as well that the boar was the sign of Diomede); and even the most sceptical person, when confronted with some evidence for such a phenomenon as a dream that predicts accurately, may have an uncomfortable feeling that there may be something in it after all.[13]

---

[10] According to Curry (p. 199), this scepticism on Pandarus' part is "assumed to comfort Troilus". Since, however, it seems thoroughly in keeping with Pandarus' character, it is not necessarily assumed, for this particular series of dreams can easily be classified as meaningless, and Pandarus need not deviate from accepted theories in order to dismiss Troilus' fears that they are prophetic.

[11] Boccaccio's Troilus knew who the boar was; cf. *Filostrato* VII, 27; Gordon, p. 110.

[12] V, 1276-1281.

[13] Again, there may be other possibilities, such as Pandarus' realization that the impressions made on Troilus by this particular dream were too strong to be dismissed with words about the general unreliability of dreams. It is, at any rate, obvious that whatever his personal feelings about the dream, Pandarus is simply trying to console and distract Troilus with his suggestion of an alternative explanation.

We can only guess at the reason behind Pandarus' different reaction to this dream, and we cannot be sure whether Chaucer meant us to understand that the dream itself is of a different variety. It is quite possibly the same kind of dream, caused by Troilus' worries; [14] but it is more specific than the other dreams, and, what is more, it is true. Cassandra's interpretation is absolutely correct. But then, we could say that the other dreams also come true, inasmuch as their general "warnings" are justified. For this reason, it does not seem to me to be correct to solve the question of the poet's intentions by classifying the earlier dream sequence as *somnium naturale* and the later dream as *somnium coeleste*. One could argue just as strongly that both dreams are prophetic, or that neither is, except by coincidence.

Of course, Criseyde's unfaithfulness is not coincidence, but an integral part of the story, and the dreams are also part of the structure of a poem. They therefore have a different function from that of a dream in real life; they are poetically true, which is still another way of looking at the question.

Aside from Troilus' dreams, there is another dream in the poem also open to several different interpretations. This is Criseyde's dream of an eagle that bears away her heart. The possible prophetic meaning is clear enough, but it is not the only feasible explanation. Her mind has been preoccupied with thoughts of the news Pandarus has brought her and with considerations of whether she will allow herself to become involved in a love affair. Therefore the dream is a true reflection of the question – if it is a question – that has had all her attention during the hours preceding the dream; it may also be a wish-fulfillment dream, since it is quite likely her unconscious desire (as we post-Freudians would say), if not her conscious wish, that Troilus should win her love.

There are a number of other dreams in Chaucer's poetry, and almost every one demonstrates an interesting facet of dream interpretation. The dream of Anelida in the fragmentary *Anelida and Arcite*, for example, demonstrates a sort of wish-fulfillment in reverse. Suspecting that her lover is false, she dreams that he is emphatically true – and finds this dream terrifying. Perhaps the dream is then a prophetic dream, to be interpreted by opposites, an interpretation which John of Salisbury tells us is common. [15] But perhaps she is merely unhappy because of the contrast between the faithful lover of her dreams and the absent one of reality; perhaps her dream is true wish-fulfillment,

---

[14]   Cf. Joseph S. Graydon, "Defense of Criseyde", *PMLA*, XLIV (1929), p. 164.
[15]   *Policraticus*, trans. Joseph B. Pike (Minneapolis, 1938), p. 82.

As if a wight hath faste a thyng in mynde,
That therof comen swiche avysiouns.[16]

Other dreams in Chaucer's poetry fit into a similar category. Thus (although it may seem a switch from the sublime to the ridiculous), Absolon in the *Miller's Tale* interprets a dream of feasting to betoken kisses, an explanation he finds highly satisfactory to his inclinations; and Sir Thopas dreams of an elf-queen, and immediately goes off in search of her. An orthodox story of dream interpretation is given by the Monk in his story of Croesus, which Chaucer condensed from the *Romance of the Rose*.[17] Also orthodox in very different ways are two dream passages in the *Squire's Tale*: Canacee's dream caused by her interest in her wonderful mirror; and the dreams of the gentlemen who had been feasting all night, which the Squire treats most contemptuously: all medical authorities agreed that the dreams that follow overindulgence in food and drink were "worthless" for prophetic purposes. Another orthodox dream interpretation is that of the Man of Law, whose heroine's sleep is disturbed by bad dreams of an unspecified nature while her mother-in-law plots to have her and her child cast out to sea.

The only "fictitious" dream in Chaucer's poetry is the one related by the Wife of Bath in her Prologue.[18] She says she is sure that the blood in the dream betokened gold and therefore good fortune, and her association of blood with gold is correct according to the dream books.[19] Gold may seem to have little to do with her real motives in telling this story to Jankyn, but, she says, this is what her mother told her to say. Because the dream is certainly startling enough, it should have accomplished its purpose: to catch Jankyn's attention.

In the *Parson's Tale* Chaucer advances still another view of dream interpretation: that it is impious. This approach views dream interpretation as a branch of sorcery, and as such it was definitely frowned on by the Church.[20] But even the Church did not take a completely

---

[16] *Troilus and Criseyde*, V, 373-374.

[17] *Roman de la Rose*, ed. Ernest Langlois (Paris, 1912), III, 7-11 (ll. 6489-6616); in the translation by F. S. Ellis (London, 1900), I, 232-236.

[18] John Barker Stearns (*Studies of the Dream as a Technical Device in Latin Epic and Drama* [Lancaster, Penna., 1927], p. 43) remarks that such dreams, "related by a character as if it had actually occurred, although in reality the character has had no such dream..." were used in literature as early as Aristophanes. (*Equites*, 1090 ff.), and that examples occur in the *Aeneid* (V, 636 ff.), in the *Argonautica* of Valerius Flaccus (i, 49 ff.), and in various works of Plautus.

[19] Cf. Curry, pp. 212 and 265.

[20] Cf. John of Salisbury, *Policraticus*, pp. 84-86.

firm stand, for, after all, the prophets of the Bible practised dream interpretation, and many of the Christian saints saw visions. The Church therefore found itself in the position of saying that it was impious to interpret dreams unless one had divine guidance – and in so saying, it tacitly expressed a faith in the divine origin of dreams.[21] Interpretation seems to have been forbidden because it is meddling with divine things, not because dreams had no meaning.

In these various instances, Chaucer explored many possible ways of explaining dreams, but at no point does he commit himself to any one view or combination of views. The *Parson's Tale* reminds us that Chaucer was a medieval Christian.[22] As such, he must have accepted to some degree the possibility of divine inspiration and guidance in dreams. However, this acceptance might not have prevented him from believing that such inspired dreams are the exception that proves the rule.

Chaucer's best known discussion of dreams occurs in the *Nun's Priest's Tale,* which contains both an example of a dream and a general discussion of the subject. The discussion of dream between Chauntecleer and Pertelote is, in a way, a summary of medieval thinking on the subject, but, though it states the arguments for the various theories of dream causes, it seems to me to be more of a re-opening of the subject than a statement of generally accepted solutions.

The dispute of Chauntecleer and Pertelote is started by Chauntecleer's reaction to his own dream. Curry considers the entire ensuing controversy to concern the classification of that dream.[23] If so, we would expect the discussion to be centered on the dream itself and on Chauntecleer's state of health, which may or may not have given rise to the dream; but this is not so. The references to dreams are to dreams *in general,* not to factors to be taken into consideration in this particular case. Pertelote, the advocate of natural causes, says "nothyng, God woot, but vanitee in sweven is".[24] This is a general statement, with no qualifications. The lines that follow do not say that *some* dreams are naturally caused, or that *many* dreams are; she states categorically that all dreams are so caused, and then goes on to apply this "fact" to

<hr>

[21] Cf. George Gordon Coulton, *Medieval Panorama: The English Scene from Conquest to Reformation* (Cambridge, England, 1938), pp. 103-118.
[22] While this tale is a faithful translation, with little added or changed by Chaucer, if Chaucer thought it important, or valid, or interesting enough to be included, it should be considered as part of his total viewpoint.
[23] Pp. 218-219.
[24] Line *4112.

his particular dream, suggesting that the red color of the beast in the dream may indicate a superfluity of red bile. Pertelote's diagnosis is as many commentators have pointed out,[25] in full accord with medieval medicine, but her position differs from accepted theories when she allows for no alternatives.[26] Chauntecleer's indignant rejoinder is equally intolerant. He, too, is sure that what he is saying is true of dreams in general, not just of a particular dream. He admits no alternative explanations: "Wher dremes be somtyme – I sey not alle – /Warnynge of thynges that shul after falle." [27] This is the only exception he allows. For, he says, many men of great authority

> han wel founden by experience
> That dremes been significaciouns
> As wel of joye as of tribulaciouns
> That folk enduren in this lif present.[28]

As for Pertelote's medicine,

> I ne telle of laxatyves no stoor,
> For they been venymous, I woot it weel;
> I hem diffye, I love hem never a deel! [29]

This, then, is a controversy over dreams in general, in which neither party takes the truly orthodox view, which, as we have seen, was that some dreams are of divine origin and others are not.[30] Naturally, the two cannot come to an agreement on the subject. Therefore any clarification of the question will have to be sought in other details of the tale.

One very important detail is the dream itself. This dream is a highly concrete vision of what actually ensues: Chauntecleer saw in his dream a beast who looked something like a dog, whose color was a shade

[25] Cf. Robinson's note, p. 753.

[26] Her quotation from Cato was used by John of Salisbury; but John applied it to only one type of dream, not to dreams in general; cf. above, p. 28. This is also quoted in *Piers Plowman* (as noted below, p. 46). Thomas A. Knott and David C. Fowler note in their edition of the A-text (Baltimore, 1952; p. 165): "Sompnia ne cures. 'Trust not dreams.' This quotation is taken from bk. II, distich 32 of *Disticha Catonis de Moribus,* an anonymous fourth-century collection of proverbs composed in the form of couplets and ascribed, during the Middle Ages, to Cato the Elder."

[27] Lines *4321-4322.

[28] Lines *4168-4171.

[29] Lines *4344-4346.

[30] Miss Mary Edith Thomas' opinion (*Chaucer and Medieval Scepticism* [New York, 1950], p. 88) that "it is Pertelote who takes the side of contemporary learned opinion" and Chauntecleer who is old-fashioned, referring to Macrobius, seems to me to fail to account for the fact that Macrobius recognized the validity of the medical view in certain cases; furthermore, the learned opinion of Chaucer's day was by no means overwhelmingly against dreams having significance for the future.

between yellow and red. The beast's tail and ears were tipped with black, his snout was small, and his eyes were bright. This is, of course, an exact description of a fox. This beast, in the dream, attacks Chauntecleer in the yard. All of this is a very literal description of the episode that follows – not a cloudy, allegorical version. The dreams in the similar *Roman de Renard* and *Reinhart der Fuchs* are both entirely allegorical, and it seems likely that the dream in whatever "original" Chaucer was following was an allegorical dream of the same family.[31] The likelihood is that Chaucer deliberately changed a figurative dream into a more specific, lifelike dream. Why? One might say because Chaucer was a realist. On the other hand, he may have intended to make the meaning of the dream all the more obvious, to make Chauntecleer the more culpable for not recognizing the danger. Chaucer's treatment of the dream removes any possibility of ambiguity – if the dream predicts future events. And, as it happens, this dream does predict future events. Everything happens just as Chauntecleer saw it in his dream.

But we cannot therefore jump to the conclusion that the moral of the tale, as Chaucer meant it, was that dreams *do* predict the future. Chaucer's humor, for one thing, must be taken into consideration. The teller of the tale, who, we must remember, is the Nun's Priest, not Chaucer himself, point out several morals, one of which is that a man should not take advice from a woman. This factor, too, was probably not in Chaucer's original: in both *Renard* and *Reinhart* it is the wife, Pinte, who interprets the dream prophetically and worries over its significance; Chauntecleer laughs it off.[32] Of this change, Nevill Coghill remarks: "Chaucer knew more of matrimony than that. It is the husband that would have high pretensions about the significance of his dreams, the wife who would pour the cold water of common sense upon them. And the wife would be wrong. . . ."[33]

But in at least one respect, Pertelote was right. She has stated that Chauntecleer's dream is "vanitee," a key word in this tale of the cock who almost loses his life because of his vanity. Chauntecleer represents

---

[31]   For varying views of Chaucer's "original", see Kate O. Petersen, *On the Sources of the Nonne Prestes Tale* (Boston, 1898), and I. C. Lecompte, "Chaucer's *Nonne Prestes Tale* and the *Roman de Renard*", MP, XIV (1916-1917), 737-749. – In both *Renard* and *Reinhart* the dream concerns a reddish fur coat with a bony opening at the throat, which the cock finds highly uncomfortable. Cf. Petersen, p. 66.
[32]   Petersen, pp. 51-55.
[33]   *The Poet Chaucer* (London, 1949), p. 155.

a tenor as well as a husband, and he has a tenor personality. He feels characteristically that any dream that *he* has *must* be important and, therefore, prophetic.

All this does not make it easy to decide whether Chaucer wanted us to reach a serious conclusion about dreams. Then, too, he futher confounds the issue with a brief but thoroughly confusing passage on free will and predestination. The train of thought of the passage runs something like this: what is ordained by God must come to pass, according to various learned clerks. Any clerk knows that this is a subject much disputed in schools. I cannot really unravel the whole thing the way Augustine or Boethius or Bishop Bradwardine could to find out whether God's foreknowing forces me to act in accordance with what is foreknown, or whether or not I have free choice to act in this way, even though God knows beforehand what I will do; or whether His knowing forces nothing except by conditional necessity. Well, concludes the Nun's Priest, I shall have nothing to do with the whole debate.

As the priest draws no conclusion, neither does Chaucer. He tells us only that the dream came true; but the dream is part of a humorous tale, and it is part and parcel of the humor that it did come true.

A number of writers, interested by Chaucer's discussions of the meaning of dreams, have attempted to decide which school of interpretation he favored. Their findings are far from unanimous. Frank Seafield finds that "Chaucer — witness, especially, the arguments *pro* and *contra* in the *Nonnes Preestes Tale* — on the whole favors the idea of divine interposition in dream-phenomena".[34] Coghill suggests that Chaucer accepted the idea that dreams were of quite different origins, and therefore that what is true of one dream is not necessarily true of another.[35] On the other hand, Huxley states: "He has no patience with superstitions. Belief in dreams, in auguries, fear of the 'raveness qualm or schrychynge of thise owles' are all unbefitting to a self-respecting man. . . ."[36] He then proceeds to quote, without any documentation, an excerpt from Pandarus' remarks to Troilus:

> To trowen on it bothe false and foul is;
> Alas, alas, so noble a creature
> As is a man shall dreden such ordure! [37]

---

[34] *Literature and Curiosities of Dreams* (London, 1865), p. 45. He is probably reading his own opinion into Chaucer; he argues for divine revelation at the end of this chapter and elsewhere.

[35] P. 49. This is also the view of Curry, as noted above (pp. 32-33).

[36] Aldous Huxley, "Chaucer", in *Essays New and Old* (New York, 1927), p. 265.

[37] *Troilus and Criseyde*, V, 383-385.

This is an example of taking words out of the mouth of one of the poet's characters and implying that they represent the opinions of the poet, when such a conclusion does not necessarily follow. Fansler, after discussing Chaucer's statements on the subject in the *House of Fame,* says: "But from other passages we may judge that Chaucer's scepticism extended to dreams as well as to alchemy, astrology, and predestination. This doubting attitude is important to bear in mind when one is considering the significance of the dream poems ... The fact that Chaucer presents Chauntecleer's dream as coming true is but another case of the poet's ironic concessions to superstitious readers." [38]

Of these statements, Fansler's is, perhaps, most nearly in accord with the evidence, but it still goes too far. It seems that the most one can say with assurance is that Chaucer did not unquestioningly accept the officially approved views, that he saw that the question was not yet settled, and that he may have felt that the solution was likely to lie in the direction of psychological and physiological explanations. The fact that Chauntecleer's dream (and other dreams, such as those of Troilus and Criseyde) came true is probably correctly ascribed to the poet's irony, but not, I think, for the reason given by Fansler. Is it not more likely that this is a sort of red herring, that the ambiguity is part of the joke? I suspect that Chaucer was, quite deliberately, being as confusing as possible about a subject he found fascinating, amusing, and unresolved.

2

The authors of the other fourteenth century dream visions give us sadly little to go on, as far as their remarks on dreams in general, or treatments of specific dreams, are concerned; they simply did not pay the extraordinary amount of attention to the subject that Chaucer did. Nevertheless, there are references to dreams in their works which should be mentioned. (I am not, of course, in this section, treating the usual remarks of the dream vision narrator to the effect that he saw all this in a dream, etc.)

Pearl has exactly one reference to a dream other than the actual dream of the narrator: the poet refers to St. John's vision of the New Jerusalem as a dream. In lines 789-792 he says:

---

[38] Dean Spruill Fansler, *Chaucer and the Roman de la Rose* (New York, 1914), p. 218.

> On þe hyl of Syon, þat semly clot,
> þe apostel hem segh in gostly drem
> Arayed to þe wedding in þat hyl-coppe,
> þe nwe cyté o Jerusalem.[39]

While he does specifically label it a "gostly" dream, it would seem that he is equating dream and vision – as, indeed, he does later in his own case, saying that his dream was a "veray avysyoun" (l. 1184). This, however, tells us nothing except that these particular dreams were divinely inspired, and that therefore the *Pearl*-poet is a believer, to some extent, in the divine nature of dreams; which is hardly surprising.

Assuming the same poet to have written *Sir Gawain and the Green Knight, Patience,* and *Purity,* we can find in these other works quite different dream references. In the section on Daniel in *Purity* we find, again not surprisingly, that Daniel is credited with the ability to interpret dreams which must, naturally, have been sent by God:

> When Nabugodenozar watz nyed in stoundes,
> He devysed his dremes to þe dere trawþe.[40]

However, a few lines earlier there is an indication that the author knew that dream interpretation was often also considered a branch of necromancy, and therefore either worthless or suspect, when he describes the

> Clerkes out of Caldye þat kennest wer knauen,
> As þe sage sathrapas þat sorsory couþe,
> Wychez and walkyries wonnen to þat sale,
> Devinores of demorlaykes þat dremes cowþe rede,
> Sorsers, and exorsismus, and fele such clerkes.[41]

This more sinister view of dream interpretation as connected with "demorlaykes", magic arts, does not, of course, in any way invalidate the divine inspiration of the dreams themselves; it was perfectly all right for Daniel, since he had the benefit of divine guidance in his interpretation.

The dreams in our hypothetical poet's other works are very definitely not of the divine type. The dreams that disturb Gawain's sleep the day before his rendezvous with the Green Knight are plainly of psychological origin:

---

[39] Ed. E. V. Gordon (Oxford, 1953), p. 29.
[40] *Purity, a Middle English Poem,* ed. Robert J. Menner (New Haven, 1920), ll. 1603-1604; p. 59.
[41] *Ibid.,* ll. 1575-1579; p. 58.

> In dreȝ drouping of dreme draueled þat noble,
> As mon þat watȝ in mornyng of mony þro þoȝtes.[42]

Similarly, Jonah, sleeping in the shade of the gourd plant, is disturbed when the Lord causes the worm to consume the plant, and wakes out of "wyl dremes", presumably caused by the physical discomfort in which he finds himself.[43]

The only conclusion we can come to, taking these four poems as the work of one man, is that the poet is aware of the theories of varying causes of dreams, and of at least one of the limitations on their interpretation. We cannot learn even that much of Langland's views from *Piers Plowman*: there is no indication at all in that poem of the existence of any kind of dream except the divinely inspired. Aside from the poet's statements about his own dream, the only dreams mentioned are those of Nebuchadnezzar, truly interpreted by Daniel,[44] and Joseph's dream of "how the mone and the sonne,/ And the elleuene sterres . hailsed hym alle",[45] which is (most surprisingly, as Skeat remarks [46]) correctly interpreted by Jacob. As far as his own dreams are concerned, the poet is very cautious, saying that he takes no pleasure in dream divination, "for I se it ofte faille" (7. 148, p. 246), and quoting our old friend "Catoun": *sompnia ne cures* (7. 150). Yet, he says, with such splendid examples as Daniel to prove that dreams *can* sometimes be interpreted, he will keep on musing about his own singular dreams. He takes a somewhat similar note in discussing his dream of the rats and the cat, but here perhaps the hesitation to interpret his dream is a bit tongue-in-cheek (to say nothing of displaying a healthy caution):

> What this meteles bemeneth . ȝe men that be merye,
> Deuine ȝe, for I ne dar . bi dere god in heuene! [47]

The view, then, expressed by Langland is that dreams seem to have meaning, if we can only find out what it is.

The anonymous poet (or poets) of the *Parliament of the Three Ages* and *Winner and Waster* has (/have) nothing to say on the subject of dreams at all, except that these poems report dreams. However, there

---

[42] *Sir Gawain and the Green Knight*, ed. J. R. R. Tolkien and E. V. Gordon (Oxford, 1955), ll. 1750-1751; p. 54.

[43] *Patience, a West Midland Poem of the Fourteenth Century*, ed. Hartley Bateson (Manchester, 1918), p. 16.

[44] Langland, *The Vision of William Concerning Piers the Plowman*, ed. Walter W. Skeat (Oxford, 1886), vol. I, p. 246; B 7. 151-158.

[45] *Ibid.*, p. 248; ll. 159-160.

[46] Vol. II, p. 129; n. to C. 10. 311.

[47] Prol., 208-209.

is another poet of the period who devoted a considerable amount of attention to dreams, John Gower. While Gower did not write any actual "dream visions",[48] a look at the dream sequences and references in the *Confessio Amantis* will help round out the picture of what the fourteenth century poets did with the subject.

Dreams often form a crucial element of the stories told in the *Confessio Amantis*. The story of Alexander includes the sinister figure of a sorcerer who has the power of "sending" dreams, Nectabanus; according to the tradition Gower was following, Alexander was actually the son of this sorcerer, who conjured up a dream to make Olympias submit to him when he subsequently appeared disguised as a god, and who also sent a dream to Philip to convince him that it had indeed been a god who impregnated his wife.[49] In Gower's version of the story of the Trojan War, the war was in effect caused by a dream, since the judgment of Paris occurs within a dream.[50] Distinctly prophetic, if somewhat veiled in allegory, are the dreams of Ulysses, conveying a warning about his son, Telegonus,[51] and of Nebuchadnezzar, whose dream is here interpreted as foreshadowing the entire history of the world, up to Gower's own time.[52] A similarly allegorical, and clearly divine, dream is the dream of the Midianite (here called a "Sarazin") which occurs in the story of Gideon.[53] An unusually clear and non-ambiguous divine dream occurs in the story of Constantine, who is instructed by Sts. Peter and Paul to go to Silvester and learn of holy writ.[54]

---

[48] It is possible that the *Confessio* itself is to be taken as a dream vision, but the situation is a bit confused. It begins with the poet as an unhappy lover walking forth in May to make his complaint to Venus and Cupid; he then sees a sort of vision of Venus and Cupid, but it is quite possibly a waking vision – he says nothing about having gone to sleep. However, in lines 154-155, he responds to Venus' initial greeting: "and I abreide/ Riht as a man doth out of slep." – *Confessio Amantis*, in *English Works*, ed. G. C. Macaulay (London, 1901), 2 vol.; all references to the *Confessio* in my text are to this edition.

[49] Part VI, ll. 1975 ff. This particular version of the birth of Alexander was most common in the Middle Ages, apparently originating with the Pseudo-Callisthenes; see Thorndike, *History of Magic and Experimental Science* (New York, 1929-1934), I, 561.

[50] Part V, 7400 ff.

[51] Part VI, 1521 ff. C. S. Lewis (*The Allegory of Love* [London, 1948], p. 210) considers the dream of Ulysses "almost among the great dreams of English poetry"; "strangely vivid because strangely ambiguous".

[52] Prol., 585 ff.; cf. I, 2785-3042, where another dream of Nebuchadnezzar is given.

[53] Part VII, 3702 ff. This is the dream related in *Judges* 7. 13.

[54] Part II, 3333 ff.

But Gower's dreams are not entirely magical or divine; there is, at least, some suggestion of other factors causing or affecting dreams. In his discussion of "Sompnolence", a subdivision of the sin of Sloth, the confessor describes the dreams which come to the sluggard:

> And of his Slouthe he dremeth ofte
> How that he stiketh in the myr,
> And how he sitteth be the fyr
> And claweth on his bare schankes,
> And how he clymbeth up the banckes
> And falleth in Slades depe.
>
> .   .   .   .
>
> And otherwhile sielde whanne
> That he mai dreme a lusti swevene,
> Him thenkth as thogh he were in hevene
> And as the world were holi his.[55]

If these dreams are in any way sent by God, God is certainly injecting a note of humor into the message. They would appear to be a combination of wish-fulfillment and accurate reflection of the state of the dreamer. In another section of the *Confessio,* the lover relates his own dreams to the confessor; they are all about love, naturally, and are either tormenting or wish-fulfilling.[56] Dreams of fulfillment are, he indicates, his only consolation.[57] Interestingly, the confessor does not remark on the patently psychological causes of these dreams, but replies that dreams are often true no matter who says the contrary! [58] He then relates the story of Ceix and Alcyone as proof.[59] This is a very peculiar answer, considering the fact that it seems obvious that the poet realized, and was making clear, the connection between the lover's waking preoccupation with unrequited love and his dreams of fulfillment or frustration. Perhaps the confessor is attempting to be consoling, but this sort of confusion, or dodging the question, is exasperatingly characteristic of Gower. One can nevertheless deduce, from this discussion and from the variety of dreams treated in Gower's work, that he saw various possible causes and functions of dreams, and he put them to remarkably good use for artistic purposes. It is interesting that no two of his dream sequences are really similar; their natures and pur-

---

[55] Part IV, 2722-2727 and 2734-2737.
[56] Part IV, 2891 ff.
[57] Part IV, 3276-3301.
[58] Part IV, 2917 ff.
[59] 2927-3123.

poses, in the lives of the dreamers or in the context of the poem, are always just a little different, so that it seems not improbable that Gower was deliberately experimenting with the possibilities of the dream.

3

It seems, then, fair to conclude that in all these cases – with the possible exception of Langland – the poets were aware of the conclusions of the "authorities" that dreams might have a variety of causes. Whether as a matter of personal conviction or for artistic purposes, a poet might take a view favoring one cause of dreams more than another, or professing his confusion on the whole subject, as Chaucer does. Clearly, the facts that the subject of dreams occurs frequently in the literature of the period, and that dreams were put to all sorts of different literary uses, shows a general interest in them. But did these poets pay much attention to the nature of the dream experience itself, beyond its causes and what Freud termed the "manifest content"? [60] That some of the literary dreams had characteristics we would still recognize today as distinctly dreamlike has been noted previously. In order to come to any final conclusions on the dreamlike qualities of dreams in Middle English poetry, we must postulate some standard of what dreamlike qualities are in general, and to do this it may be helpful to look at the conclusions of modern psychology, and see how they agree with medieval theory and practice.

[60] Sigmund Freud, *The Interpretation of Dreams*, in *Basic Writings*, trans. A. A. Brill (New York, 1938), p. 218, *et passim*.

IV

DEFINING THE DREAM: MODERN LIGHT ON AN ANCIENT PROBLEM

No reader of this post-Freudian age can have failed to notice in the foregoing discussion of medieval dream theories that many of the ideas on dream interpretation we consider "modern" were quite familiar in the Middle Ages, and are no fresh invention of the twentieth century. Freud himself, who can be called the founder of modern dream psychology, acknowledged this fact in several different connections. In his summary of the history of dream interpretation, he noted that many of the ancients recognized the possibility that dreams could aid in the diagnosis of physical and psychic ailments;[1] he bowed to the poets' grasp of the way ideas present themselves in dreams;[2] and he acknowledged the basic correctness of the age-old idea that dreams have a symbolic meaning, an idea which had been attacked and rejected by the science of the nineteenth century. Of this "modern" viewpoint, he remarked (p. 191): "I have, however, come to think differently. I have been forced to perceive that here, once more, we have one of those not infrequent cases where an ancient and stubbornly retained popular belief seems to have come nearer to the truth of the matter than the opinion of modern science. I must insist that the dream actually does possess a meaning, and that a scientific method of dream-interpretation is possible."

This statement, a sort of basic manifesto of modern dream theory, emphasizes the fact that we can and should take "popular belief" seriously; a view with which other branches of modern medicine have increasingly come into accord, and a view accepted and adopted by Freud's followers and successors in this particular field, whether or not they agree with all of his conclusions. One recent textbook on dream interpretation, Werner-Wolff's *The Dream – Mirror of Conscience*,[3]

[1] *The Interpretation of Dreams,* in *Basic Writings,* trans. A. A. Brill (New York, 1938), p. 184.
[2] *Ibid.,* p. 189.
[3] (New York, 1952).

a book written by a psychologist for students of psychology and psychiatry, devotes considerable space to a history of man's thought over the ages on the subject of dreams, finding a great deal of significance and value in all the ways in which men have tried to explain the nature and meaning of dreams. Wolff's object is, in part, to point out the universality of certain conceptions, and the resemblance of seemingly different ideas held by cultures widely separated in time and space. To the student of medieval dream philosophy, a particularly striking example of this is evident in Wolff's own analysis of the nature of the various statements about, and examples of, dreams in the Bible. His division of these Biblical dream references into types bears a startling resemblance to the categories of Macrobius and John of Salisbury.[4] Corresponding to Macrobius' categories of *oraculum* and *visio*, the Bible has, of course, a number of dreams said to be inspired by God. Man may ask a favor of God, and thus "configurate" his destiny (*I Kings* 3). He may receive "clues for action" (*Gen.* 31: 11). A dream may be prophetic, revealing the future of the dreamer, but difficult, if not impossible, of interpretation (*Gen.* 37: 5 ff., 40: 9-19, 41: 32); or it may be spiritual, of the future (*Joel* 2: 28). There are nightmares (*Job* 7: 14), which could fall under Macrobius' category of *insomnium*, and illusory, lying dreams (*Jeremiah* 23: 32, 23: 28, 29: 8), corresponding to Macrobius' *visium*. Two types of Biblical dreams round out the categories, falling into the *somnium* type; these are wish-fulfillment (*Isaiah* 29: 8) and reflection of recent activity (*Ecclesiastes* 5: 3). "There is no new thing under the sun", said Ecclesiastes; a statement once more borne out by the fact that Macrobius could have found a Biblical precedent for every one of his categories, as well as the fact that psychologists of the twentieth century are still finding "new" truths in ancient and medieval theories.

The earliest modern pronouncement on the nature of the dream would have caused no ripple of surprise in the fourteenth century: a dream, said Freud, is the fulfillment of a wish.[5] The only way in which this pronouncement differs from medieval theory is in its insistence that the dream is *always* the fulfillment of a wish, never anything else, no matter how far from our conscious wishes the tenor of the dream may seem to be. But most of Freud's successors would also take issue with this limitation of dream purpose. Some have developed alternative all-encompassing theories; Wolff's final opinion is that we synthesize

---

[4] See pp. 13-15.
[5] *Op. cit.*, p. 205 ff.

our experience in sleep, seeking for solutions of various sorts. This could mean a type of wish-fulfillment in many cases, but it is not necessarily that simple. He feels that because of this synthetic function dreams may anticipate or prognosticate the future; he even admits telepathy as possible.[6] On the other hand, Jung, who has undoubtedly been the most influential figure in the field next to Freud, states flatly that he works on the principle that there is "no general theory of dreams".[7] As Ira Progoff remarks, "he does have a theory of dreams", and it so happens that "the dreams which he reconstructs tend to fit the pattern of his general approach to psychic phenomena";[8] but Jung is ready to recognize the possibility of dreams being wish-fulfillment, among other possibilities. He states: "The view that dreams are merely imaginary fulfillments of suppressed wishes has long ago been superseded. It is certainly true that there are dreams which embody suppressed wishes and fears, but what is there which the dream cannot on occasion embody? Dreams may give expression to ineluctable truths, to philosophical pronouncements, illusions, wild fantasies, memories, plans, anticipations, irrational experiences, even telepathic visions, and heaven knows what besides."[9]

At this time, then, we can only say that the causes and implications of dreams are manifold; the main way in which the conclusions along this line of the modern psychologists are apt to differ from those of medieval investigators of the field is that we speak of "the unconscious", rather than of "the supernatural". Jung remarks: "Formerly it [the dream] was esteemed as a harbinger of fate, a portent and comforter, a messenger of the gods. Now we see it as the emissary of the unconscious, whose task it is to reveal the secrets that are hidden from the conscious mind, and this it does with astounding completeness."[10] This is almost a matter of terminology; the two views are far from irreconcilable.

Since, in a sense, the twentieth century has reconfirmed, if re-defined, what the fourteenth century knew about dream causation, let us look at the conclusions of our psychologists on the actual workings of the

---

[6] *Ibid.*, p. 223.
[7] C. G. Jung, *The Integration of the Personality*, trans. S. M. Dell (New York, 1939), p. 98.
[8] *Jung's Psychology and Its Social Meaning* (New York, 1955), p. 136.
[9] *Modern Man in Search of a Soul*, trans. W. S. Dell and Cary F. Baynes (New York, 1933), p. 11.
[10] "On the Psychology of the Unconscious", in *Two Essays on Analytical Psychology*, trans. R. F. C. Hull (New York, 1956), pp. 30-31.

dream itself. Medieval dream literature took up this aspect only insofar as it assigned a fixed meaning to symbols and events seen in the dream; this is the sort of thing found in many a medieval dream book, the lore on which the Wife of Bath relied in her encounter with Jankyn. An interpretation of symbols according to a fixed one-to-one correspondence is by no means unknown to modern science; [11] this aspect, however, will be taken up a little later, since modern theories on the subject can only be understood in light of the "dream-work", which was first defined by Freud.

It was Freud's contention that there were two distinctly separate layers of "content" in a dream, the "manifest" content – the exact impressions retained in the memory – and the "latent" content, the dream-thoughts which gave rise to, and are both expressed in and concealed by, the manifest content. "The dream-content," he explained (p. 319), "appears to us as a translation of the dream-thought into another mode of expression, whose symbols and laws of composition we must learn by comparing the original with the translation. . . . The dream-content is, as it were, presented in hieroglyphics, whose symbols must be translated, one by one, into the language of the dream-thoughts." With this basic assumption, he proceeded to define just what had happened to the latent dream-thoughts in the various particular dreams he had analyzed, and reached two main conclusions which have been accepted, in essence if not in detail, by everyone since his time: the two obvious characteristics of the 'dream-work" are condensation and displacement.

Condensation implies, first, a compression of many ideas into a few symbols. 'The dream, when written down, fills half a page, the analysis, which contains the dream-thoughts, requires six, eight, twelve times as much space. The ratio varies with different dreams; but in my experience it is always of the same order." [12] Demonstrating how this works by citing some of his own dreams, he showed that a single person in a dream could combine characteristics of several people, forming a "collective image" having little to do with the person presumably in question, but significantly concerning any number of other people, who are, for some reason or other – no matter how obscure the connection may seem – related in the dreamer's mind to the characteristics of the person ostensibly present in the dream. This may be a shifting matter

[11] As a matter of fact, Dame Alys's relation of gold to blood is highly significant in the Freudian system; cf., *The Interpretation of Dreams*, pp. 375 and 397.
[12] Freud, p. 320.

– one personality fading out as another takes over – or it may be a more stable "composite person", in which the dream-image is a definite combination of traits of two or more persons superimposed upon each other.

Condensation is not, of course, limited to persons. Events in dreams can likewise be shown to refer to more than one event or idea; and, most interestingly, words themselves, either as they occur in the dream or as the dreamer later relates them to the remembered dream content, can be shown to condense two or more meanings or associations. Freud's dream analysis places a particular emphasis on this matter of what he terms "word formation" and "verbal transformations".[13] These processes produce a type of word-play that is scarcely to be distinguished from the waking – or literary – "pun" and the sort of "portmanteau word" for which Lewis Carroll is so justly famous. In this respect, the connection between the ways of the dreaming mind and the "wit" of the conscious mind are quite obviously related, as Freud pointed out in *Wit and Its Relation to the Unconscious*.[14]

By "displacement", Freud meant primarily that the true contents of the dream may be expressed through entirely different elements: "That which is obviously the essential content of the dream-thoughts need not be represented at all in the dream. The dream is, as it were, *centred elsewhere*; its content is arranged about elements which do not constitute the central point of the dream-thoughts" (p. 336). This transference naturally causes a distortion in the dream content, as does the concomitant "condensation". Displacement, too, may be verbal, according to Freud: here he found examples of an image, or picture, in a dream which seems quite meaningless, until it is translated into language and found to be a pun, or some such play on words, referring to something of real importance to the dreamer.[15]

These two aspects of "dream-work" have been further explored and defined by Freud's followers. A recent textbook on dream analysis discusses these mechanisms, and their refinements, as "condensation", "splitting of the symbol", "changing situations", and "split of the ego".[16] "Changing situations" is, of course, actually just one of the aspects of condensation, which is here defined as "similar objects or ideas ... condensed and fused into unities". "Splitting of the symbol"

[13]   Cf. especially pp. 331-336.
[14]   In *Basic Writings*, pp. 633-803; see especially pp. 745-761.
[15]   See, e.g., pp. 361-365.
[16]   Emil A. Gutheil, *The Handbook of Dream Analysis* (New York, 1951), pp. 111 ff., 178-185.

involves showing one person or object represented by two or more, which is certainly a form of displacement, under which category "split of the ego", a projection of some aspect of the personality onto another, also would come. Another psychologist is dealing with a similar distinction when he says that "any dream is either a *reduction* or an *elaboration* of its underlying thoughts".[17]

Where many later psychologists would leave Freud is in his theory of the cause of these phenomena, the theory of the "dream censor". If, as Freud maintained, all dreams are a form of wish-fulfillment, then the "dream censor" appears to be a logical conclusion; how else can we hold that dreams, or elements in dreams, which appear to be absolute nonsense are fulfilling a wish, unless there is some reason why this wish cannot be more directly expressed? The absurdity of dreams, Freud held, represented a sort of criticism or consolation (p. 409 ff.). Jung summarizes this position, saying: "According to Freud, the painful and incompatible elements in the conflict are in this way so covered up or obliterated that we may speak of a 'wish-fulfillment.'"[18] But, as we have already seen, many psychologists today feel that wish-fulfillment is only *one* of the possible functions of the dream; therefore the concept of the dream censor is of only limited usefulness. Jung's ideas about the "collective unconscious", a sort of racial memory expressed through symbols which he calls "archetypes", would indicate quite a different function for the dream-work of condensation and displacement, one of revelation rather than obfuscation. In his view, certain ideas of great importance to the individual and to the race can only be expressed through these symbols; thus, the confusing or confused symbolism of dreams may be the best way of expressing a truth, a way in which the contents of the "unconscious" can break through into the conscious mind, as opposed to a deliberate attempt on the part of one segment of the mind to pacify another without revealing a painful truth.

These two points of view work out rather paradoxically in their author's application of them to the actual symbols found in dreams. Freud, whose basic tenet here is that "the representation effected by the dream-work ... *was never even intended to be understood*" (p. 362), nevertheless comes to the conclusion that a great many recurrent elements in dreams have a very definite significance in the majority of cases. He states, for example: "Small boxes, chests, cupboards, and ovens correspond to the female organ; also cavities, ships, and all kinds

[17] Wolff, p. 311.
[18] "On the Psychology of the Unconscious", p. 31.

of vessels. – A room in a dream generally represents a woman; the description of its various entrances and exits is scarcely calculated to make us doubt this interpretation" (p. 371). Anyone who has read through the catalog of Freud's "symbols" is aware that there is scarcely an innocent object or familiar dream situation for which he does not find such a correspondence. He does, however, qualify these statements with the remark that these things may vary in different contexts, and, furthermore, notes that not everything is to be interpreted symbolically, saying (p. 362): "Generally speaking, in the interpretation of any element of a dream it is doubtful whether it (a) is to be accepted in the negative or the positive sense (contrast relation); (b) is to be interpreted historically (as a memory); (c) is symbolic; or whether (d) its valuation is to be based upon its wording."

Jung, on the other hand, in spite of his theory of "archetypes", maintains that the symbols emanating from the "unconscious", including those of dreams, do not have a fixed meaning, but must always be interpreted in context. Progoff says, summing up Jung's position: "It depends always on the dream, and particularly on the dreamer. . . . It is incorrect to say that any given object or figure necessarily has the same significance when it appears in the dream of one individual as when it appears in the dream of another." [19] But it must still be remembered that Jung does find universal significance in the various forms of the "archetypes"; the "magic demon", for example, who, he says, may appear in many forms, including that of the "wise old man." [20] Further discussion here of the nature of Jung's "archetypes" would seem unnecessary, in view of the extensive literature on the subject, particularly the work of Maud Bodkin, whose *Archetypal Patterns in Poetry* is well known to students of literary criticism.

In current psychological literature it remains something of a question to what extent dream symbols have a similar connotation in the dreams of different individuals. There is, however, no question that the dream is largely symbolic, and some of the later writers have some interesting theories and observation to add on the subject of dream symbolism. Werner Wolff, in line with his overall theory of the synthetic function

[19] *Op. cit.*, p. 138.
[20] "On the Psychology of the Unconscious", pp. 106-107. Cf. the "wind" archetype discussed in "The Relations Between the Ego and the Unconscious", in *Two Essays*, pp. 141-147. The connection of "wind" with "spirit", and therefore with God, is philologically obvious, and well-known to students of theology; but this particular point seems especially noteworthy to the student of Langland, in view of the "high wind" in *Piers Plowman*.

of dreams, defines the dream symbol as the "fusion of many ideas into one pattern" (p. 310), which would make it a result of what Freud termed condensation. He goes on to maintain that dream images "picture what they mean" (p. 311); they are what they seem to be, as well as (instead of supplanting, as in Freud) what they suggest by comparison. Therefore, says Wolff, a dream may have "various meanings at the same time". In any terms, interpreting these symbols remains a highly complex business; Nandor Fodor emphasizes this when he remarks: "Associations may move on many levels: personal and impersonal, past and present, farcical and serious; intellectual and emotive, regressive and progressive, deceptive and genuine, mature and infantile. Room should also be found for advance, telepathic and precognitive associations." [21]

In some ways, these contemporary theories on the workings of the dream, and the meaning of dream symbolism, would seem to be something quite different from anything medieval students of the subject had to say. Nobody today would agree with Gregory of Nyssa that the absurdity of the dream is produced by an absence of intellect, and that the images produced by memory come up in the dream state by sheer chance.[22] But psychologists would probably agree that the fourth century commentator was on the right track: the *waking* intellect is certainly absent, and it is precisely the absence of the conscious level of the mind which allows another type of logic, the unconscious or whatever we wish to call it, to take over. As Erich Fromm puts it, "The unconscious is the mental experience in a state of existence in which we have shut off communications with the outer world, are no longer preoccupied with action but with our self-experience." [23] Similarly, it is possible to find a medieval precedent for almost all the various facets of our dream theory; even Jung's theory of the "collective unconscious" has an ancestry going back, perhaps, to the neo-Platonic ideas of a "world mind". St. Thomas Aquinas, who believed that dreams might cause future events, advanced the theory that possibly dreams and future events did not cause each other, but were both the product of some "third agency"; Albertus Magnus, agreeing with Aquinas, termed this "third agency" "the universal sense". It was his idea that all things are in some way related, and that it is the function of part

[21] *New Approaches to Dream Interpretation* (New York, 1951), p. vii.
[22] "Gregory of Nyssa", in *The Ante-Nicene Fathers*, vol. II, trans. Peter Holmes (New York, 1918); cf. Wolff, p. 24.
[23] *The Forgotten Language: An Introduction to the Understanding of Dreams, Fairy Tales and Myths* (New York, 1951), p. 29.

of the brain to transform impressions into images – a theory which is certainly right in line with much twentieth century thought.[24] Another aspect of Jung's theory involves the distinction between individual and social dreams, a concept which he noted among savages, who distinguished between the "ordinary dream of the little man, and the 'big visions' that only the great man has, e.g., the medicine-man or chief".[25] To Jung, of course, this means the difference between the significant dream which springs from the collective unconscious and one involving only immediate personal interests; but the distinction certainly has a most familiar ring to the student of Macrobius, who made just such a distinction between dreams of private and public significance.

Nevertheless, if we are going to bear these theories, formulated in our own time, in mind as we examine poetry of an earlier period, caution is obviously necessary; there is a double jeopardy – the danger that we will refuse to believe that a poet who never heard of Freud or Jung could have had a similar insight into the workings of the dreaming mind, and the danger that we will insist that he must have. Jung himself has been careful to point out the danger of *reducing* poetic symbolism to archetypes; the archetype, embodying a universal human truth, may indeed be there, but, he says, if we look just for that, we may miss the real meaning of the symbol, which deals also with something more specific.[26] But he also emphasizes that the very nature of these archetypal images is such that they may be in a work without the artist's having consciously meant them to be there; in this connection, he remarks that one of the reasons for the sudden "rediscovery" of long-dead poets is that their work may be based on symbols which speak more to one time than another.[27] Jung even goes so far as to suggest that in the case of what he terms "visionary" literature, poets are apt to deliberately deny the un-realistic (in the sense of "everyday" realism) nature of their material; but, he says, "the truth is that poets are human beings, and that what a poet has to say about his work is often far from being the most illuminating word on the subject".[28]

---

[24]   St. Thomas Aquinas, *Summa Theologica*, trans. by Fathers of the English Dominican Province, Part II (London, 1922), p. 204; Albertus Magnus, *Being the Approved, Verified, Sympathetic and Natural Egyptian Secrets,* ed. L. W. de Laurence (Chicago, 1910); Wolff, p. 25.
[25]   "The Relations Between the Ego and the Unconscious", p. 187.
[26]   "On the Relationship of Analytical Psychology to Poetic Art", in *Contributions to Analytical Psychology* (London, 1928), p. 232.
[27]   *Ibid.,* p. 241.
[28]   *Modern Man in Search of a Soul,* p. 161.

That there is, and always has been, a very real connection between the type of symbolism found in poetry and that of dreams, and a similarity between the way in which a dream works and a work of art, is one of the most frequently reiterated conclusions of psychologists. Miss Maud Bodkin, demonstrating the resemblances between a dream embodying an unmistakable "rebirth" experience through water and various poetic uses of water as a symbol of death and new life, seems quite reasonable and downright conservative in drawing the conclusion that "the forces of our sensibility find expression, in a manner somewhat parallel, within the imagery of dream and of poetry".[29] Then, besides the correspondence between the specific types of imagery used in both dream and poetry, many other important resemblances have been noted between the dream-work and the work of the poet. Just as he regards the dream as an attempt of the mind to assimilate material from the unconscious with the conscious level of the mind, Jung describes the poet as using materials from the subconscious under conscious control, assimilating it within the bounds of "contemporary consciousness".[30] Of the finished products, he has a very interesting comment: "A great work of art is like a dream; for all its apparent obviousness it does not explain itself and is never unequivocal. A dream never says: 'You ought', or: 'This is the truth'. It presents an image in much the same way as nature allows a plant to grow, and we must draw our own conclusions." [31]

Another resemblance suggested by an early Freudian is the way in which a multitude of associations are collected around a possibly trivial incident in both poetry and dream: "In dreams we have seen that some incident of the preceding day, which is free of associations, serves as a starting point or point of crystallization. So the inspired poet often finds in some casual experience – a mountain daisy . . . – a centre around which his poetic conceptions may gather." [32]

We know, then, that there are many resemblances between the poet at work and the dreaming mind, and between the poem and the dream. But did the poets of the fourteenth century know this? We do not know of any medieval analysis of the work of the dream that is comparable to modern analyses of dream-work, or any statement that can be construed as referring to the phenomena of condensation and dis-

[29] *Archetypal Patterns in Poetry* (New York, 1958), p. 65.
[30] "On the Relationship of Analytical Psychology to Poetic Art", p. 232.
[31] *Modern Man in Search of a Soul*, pp. 171-172.
[32] F. C. Prescott, *Poetry and Dreams* (Boston, 1919), p. 43.

placement, except for the common acknowledgment that dreams may be meant to be interpreted "by opposites". Still, the main reason why such modern analyses are convincing is the simple fact that they are in accordance with what we all know from our own experience, if we have given that experience any thought. This experience was just as much part of the life of men in the fourteenth century as it is today, and it would certainly seem very odd indeed if men as interested in the phenomena of dreams as Chaucer and Gower, for example, most certainly were had not noticed the peculiarities of their dream experiences. Freud was sure that this was the cause throughout the ages, and that the peculiarities of the dreaming state are to be found in almost all dream poetry. He stated: "Most of the artificial dreams contrived by poets are intended for some such symbolic interpretation, for they reproduce the thought conceived by the poet in a guise not unlike the disguise which we are wont to find in our dreams." [33]

It would hardly seem rash to assume, in the light of all this, that when we find resemblances in Middle English dream poetry to what we can understand as the actual dreaming state, this is not necessarily a coincidence. We know that dreams were a topic of great interest to our poets, and that medieval theories on the nature of dreams were not so very distant from our own. It may prove fruitful to bear these facts in mind as we come to examine the purposes of the dream in Middle English poetry, especially when it is used as a "form" in itself.

[33] *The Interpretation of Dreams*, p. 189.

V

TWO DREAM ELEGIES:
PEARL AND THE *BOOK OF THE DUCHESS*

Critics of medieval poetry have for some time been aware that the poets made some use of dream psychology in the dream visions; the question is not whether this is so, but to what extent this is so. The only Middle English dream vision which has been really thoroughly considered from this point of view is Chaucer's *Book of the Duchess*; but the existence of a psychological element has been at least noted in other poems. Gordon, remarking on the demand for "authority" in medieval literature, remarked: "This was one of the reasons for the popularity of visions: they allowed marvels to be placed within the real world, linking them with a person, a place, a time, while providing them with an explanation in the phantasies of sleep, and a defence against critics in the notorius deception of dreams." [1] This suggests that the poet may use the well-known fact that dreams could have psychological origins as a sort of anchor out to windward, an addition to his claim to divine authority. In using the dream vision form, the poet can call upon an excellent motivating device, since, as Chaucer remarked,

> The wery huntere, slepynge in his bed,
> To wode ayeyn his mynde goth anon;
> The juge dremeth how his plees been sped;
> The cartere dremeth how his cartes gon;
> The riche, of gold; the knyght fyght with his fon;
> The syke met he drynketh of the tonne;
> The lovere met he hath his lady wonne. [2]

Pearl is a case in point. The *Pearl*-poet uses just such a dream motivation: the bereaved "jeweler" falls asleep grieving for his "pearl", and

---

[1] Introduction to *Pearl* (Oxford, 1953), pp. xiv-xv. – All references to the poem in my text are from this edition.
[2] *Parliament of Fowls*, ll. 99-105.

quite naturally dreams of the pearl.[3] The connection is in perfect accord with dream psychology, whether medieval or modern; if it were not so, there would be less room for doubt in the minds of the critics as to whether the poem is primarily an elegy or primarily a didactic poem. The psychological aspect does not, however, destroy the poet's claim to have his poem regarded as a divine vision. The dream was, he suggests, a vision sent to comfort and instruct him, and he maintains that it is a "veray avysyoun" (l. 1184). The psychological motivation is an addition to the dream concept, rather than an alternative explanation, and it provides the poet with a framework which is both plausible to his audience and artistically helpful.[4]

The dream convention is most obviously accommodating to the poet as an excuse for the inclusion of a great deal of didactic material. The confusion and lack of logic, by waking standards, of the dreaming mind provided an acceptable reason for the poet to portray himself as extraordinarily dense and confused. As Earle Birney remarks in a discussion of the "daswed" dreamer in Chaucer's *Book of the Duchess*: "This was consistent both with psychological realism and with medieval literary practice; the author represents himself as wrong-headed and dull to facilitate a story or sermon from the wise and loquacious teacher encountered in the vision. The teacher must be furnished a pupil obviously in need of advice or ignorant of what is probably a familiar story."[5] The *Pearl*-poet avails himself of this opportunity, perhaps all too thoroughly. The dreamer is told several times that he may not pass the river (e.g., l. 299), yet he keeps forgetting and trying again. After the Pearl has given a complete explanation of her position in heaven in lines 413 ff., he asks the same questions all over again in slightly different form. The dreamer's assumption in lines 919-922 that the Pearl is referring to the "old" Jerusalem, rather than the New Jerusalem of *Revelation,* shows another sort of confusion – and is equally exasperating. But all of this affords an opportunity for the Pearl to enlighten the dreamer, and also serves to advance the "plot" of the poem. For example, the dreamer's initial questions on his Pearl's social status

[3] The dream is further tied to waking reality by the fact that it occurs on the day of the Assumption of the Virgin, when the poet's mind might have been turned to thoughts along these lines. (For the argument identifying the date as the day of this feast, see C. G. Osgood's introduction to his edition of *Pearl* [Boston, 1906], p. xvi.)

[4] The view that one can believe any or all of the allegorical interpretations proposed and still accept the historicity of the child has been ably set forth by Jefferson B. Fletcher, "The Allegory of the Pearl", *JEGP*, XX (1921), 1-21.

[5] "The Beginnings of Chaucer's Irony", *PMLA*, LIV (1939), p. 645.

elicited a complete doctrinal explanation, but when he asks again it provides an occasion for the vision of the New Jerusalem.

Aside from the bemused condition of the dreamer, there are many other suggestions of the peculiar world of dreams in *Pearl*. It would be going too far to expect that all of these suggestions were deliberately worked out by the poet with the specific intention of conveying characteristics of the dream state; but, being there, they contribute to whatever claim the poem has to be regarded as a dream. One of these factors is the sharply visual quality of the poem. The marvelous countryside, the birds and the leaves, the Pearl herself, and the Holy City are all described in very vivid fashion, with loving attention to detail and color. This may not be markedly different from the poet's waking observation, but it is dreamlike in that, as we have noted, dreams tend to be largely visual.[6]

More subtle indications of dream psychology are also present. We find ourselves doing things in dreams which are physically impossible, or at least painful, in reality; just so, the dreaming poet is surprised to find how easily he moves about and climbs the hills in his dream: "No bonk so byg þat did me dereʒ" (l. 102). Conversely, we may "freeze" in a dream and find that try as we may we cannot move, and the effort to move may be what rouses us from the dream. This happens in *Pearl*, too, when the dreamer makes his effort to cross the stream and cannot, but wakes. The people we meet in dreams are often completely different from their real prototypes, and yet we know who they are, just as the dreamer of *Pearl* recognizes his pearl at once, although the grown young lady can bear little resemblance to an infant not yet two years old ("þou lyfed not two ʒer in our þede", l. 483). Again, in waking life it would hardly be possible for a man to stand on a hill and see every individual in a distant city, but distance melts away in a dream, and the dreamer does just that. Also dreamlike is the fact that the dreamer is only mildly surprised when he sees the maiden who was right by his side a moment ago appear as one of the throng in the city.

Again, the central theme of the poem is not the only reflection of the dreamer's waking preoccupations. The dream contains elements which pick up and echo, in a suitably metamorphosed form, various minor aspects of the dreamer's pre-sleeping consciousness. The dreamer went to sleep in a garden, and dreamt of a garden with certain similarities, yet all changed into a dream world. The waking garden contained a "huyle þer perle hit trendeled doun" (l. 41), and the dream garden

6 Cf. above, p. 18.

is set in much greater hills with crystal cliffs. In that real garden the dreamer has heard (or composed?) sweet songs; songs recur constantly in the dream, both the song of the birds (l. 94) and the heavenly songs of the blessed (ll. 879 ff., 1124). The song in the earthly garden, and the poet's memory of the lost pearl, make the frame of mind in which he falls asleep not entirely desolate, but rather bittersweet; just so, the consolation of the dream is bittersweet, blending joy and anguish, and this ambivalence is even echoed in the words of the poem, in the reiteration of the words "bliss" and "bale".[7]

Quite a few of the poet's more remarkable ways of using language are strikingly appropriate to the dreaming state. One of the better-known characteristics of the dream is that people, places, and things in general blend and fuse. Two different figures may represent one, or, on the other hand, one figure may combine aspects of several. The language of *Pearl* is curiously in accordance with this characteristic.[8] Many words are used with emphasis on shifting meanings; often the key word of a stanza group is used with two or more separate meaning; as, for example, "spot" (stanza group I), "deme" (VI), "date" (IX), "mote" (XVI), and "mone" (XVIII). This is underlined by the pairing of distinctly different words which echo each other in sound although not in meaning, such as "maskeleȝ" and "makeleȝ", the key words of stanza group XIII, and "now" and "inoghe" in stanza group XI. The very verse form is characterized by blending and fusion, in its linking of stanzas and stanza groups through key words.

Just as the meaning of words shifts constantly, so, it would appear, does the meaning or application of various images and symbols in the dream. The all-pervasive pearl is used as a symbol for the child who has died, the redeemed and glorified soul of the child maiden,[9] and her purity and her state of blessedness. Further, as Gordon said, "these significations are extended to the other pearls in the poem. The maiden's raiment is sewn with them in token of her innocence; her pinnacled crown of pure white pearl is the privilege of her heavenly blessedness; the large and lustrous pearl she wears on her breast, we are told, is none other than the pearl of price that the merchant of Christ's parable gave all his goods to buy ... Each gate of the Heavenly City is made of one single unfading pearl" (p. xxviii).[10] Moreover, Henry R. Rupp

---

[7]   In particular, cf. ll. 371-374.

[8]   Cf. Freud, *Wit and the Unconscious*; cited above (p. 54, n. 14).

[9]   Cf. Dante's *Paradiso*, XXII 22-30, where the soul of St. Benedict appears as a pearl.

[10]   Rabanus Maurus (in Migne, *Pat. Lat.*, CXII [Paris, 1878], col. 996) lists as

remarks that the "jewels" of the lady's "sawes" in lines 277-278 may be meant to be understood as "pearls," and that possibly we may be meant to consider her as throwing her pearls before swine, since the dreamer seems to be unable to grasp most of her instruction.[11]

Still another pearl metaphor which may be implicit in the poem is suggested by J. P. Oakden, who draws attention to the passage in *Purity* (ll. 1115-1132) which states that a man can be cleansed of his sins through shrift and penance just as a pearl which has lost its color may be restored by washing it in wine.[12] The Pearl states that the Lamb washed her "wede" in his blood (l. 766), which could indeed suggest the washing of a pearl in wine. If this metaphor is implied, then the multifold pearl imagery blends right into another group of images, those concerned with blood and water, which suggest, among other things, the traditional separation of the "other world", baptism, the blood shed by Christ on the cross, and the mass.[13] The river is both death and the water of life, and God's mercy is described as being like "water of dyche/ oþer goteȝ of golf þat neuer charde" (ll. 607-608). Like the pearl symbolism, water images and other images used in the poem are constantly shifting, kaleidoscopic.[14] In a similar way, there might be some dream justification for the fact that various descriptions from the Bible are transposed and mixed. The merging of the innocents

---

two of the meanings of the pearl desire of the Kingdom of Heaven (*Matt.* xiii, 46) and "*homines justi*", who, he says, are the gates of heaven of *Rev.* xxi. 21; i.e., the faith through which they enter heaven.

[11] Other meanings attached to pearls by various medieval writers have been pointed out by various scholars; they include: earthly delights (*Rev.* xvii, the ornaments of the Whore of Babylon); healing; Christ; the saints; God's grace; the faith of the Church; the mystery of the Resurrection; the Church as the Mystical Body of Christ. For a summary of most of these, see René Wellek, "The Pearl", *Studies in English*, IV, *Charles University* (Prague, 1933), 5-33; cf. also Osgood's introduction to *Pearl*; R. M. Garrett, "The Pearl: An Interpretation", *Univ. of Wash. Pub. in Eng.*, IV, no. 1 (April, 1918); and S. K. Heninger, Jr., "The Margarite-Pearl Allegory in Thomas Usk's *Testament of Love*", *Speculum*, XXXII (1957), 92-98.

[12] *Alliterative Poetry in Middle English* (Manchester, 1935), II, p. 75.

[13] One interesting connection between the pearl, as a symbol, and the mass, is that, according to Rabanus Maurus (col. 995), the pearl was engendered by dew; as manna was also supposed to have been engendered by dew, and as manna is symbolic, in the anagogical sense, of the mass, the pearl is therefore symbolic of the mass. Cf. Heninger, pp. 97-98; Garrett, pp. 17-23.

[14] On the various gemological and botanic images, cf. Milton R. Stern, "An Approach to *The Pearl*", *JEGP*, LIV (1955), pp. 684-692. Stern develops the parallels between the gemological meanings of the foundation stones of the Heavenly City and the stages of the jeweler's progress, and also notes the particular significance of the spices mentioned.

and the virgins, and the assignment of the raiment of the symbolic bride of Christ, the Church, to the Pearl, could be a blending along the same lines as the blending of imagery and language.

The dreamlike characteristics of the poem add to its singular impression of polished perfection in several ways. It is characteristic of the *Pearl*-poet that there are no loose ends; any one element of his poem may serve two purposes, and thus connect various aspects. The dream concept itself serves to connect the elegiac theme with the doctrinal content of the poem in such a close connection that they are virtually inseparable.[15] The constantly changing and blending symbolism allows the poet to deepen and enrich his discussion at the same time that it helps maintain the effect of a dream. The same thing is true of the poet's use of language, which in addition underlines and harmonizes with his use of symbols.

Sisam remarks that the effect of *Pearl* is "highly wrought, almost overwrought",[16] and that "the form distracts attention from the matter by its elaborateness" (p. 58). It is indeed highly wrought; but this really seems to be the special excellence of *Pearl*, rather than a drawback. The admirable symmetry of the poem, and its wonderful appropriateness of language and style to theme and form, call forth our admiration for the total effect while they simultaneously offer us a fascinating complexity, in which we are forever discovering new and heretofore unnoticed subtleties. There is nothing sloppy about the poem, but it is far from such straightforward simplicity that he may run who readeth it.

The *Pearl*-poet has made maximum use of the dream as a unifying device, as well as a way of lending weight to a highly serious subject, at the same time pacifying the authority-minded medieval audience, to whom a frank fiction would probably have been equivalent to a lie, and undeserving of serious attention.

Blending, fusion, and double-meaning have all been seen to be characteristic of *Pearl,* and of dreams. I believe it can be shown that these phenomena, amounting to much the same thing as Freud's "condensation" and "displacement", are also observable in other Middle English dream visions, and that they are, in fact, a significant earmark of the

---

[15] Cf. Gordon, pp. xviii-xix: "Without the elegiac basis and the sense of great personal loss which pervades it, *Pearl* would indeed be the mere theological treatise on a special point, which some critics have called it. But without the theological debate the grief would never have risen above the ground."
[16] *Fourteenth Century Verse and Prose*, ed. Kenneth Sisam (Oxford, 1955), p. 59.

form in this period. This does not, however, imply that they are always used in the same way as in *Pearl*. This is obvious when we compare *Pearl* to the *Book of the Duchess,* Chaucer's earliest dream vision. In many ways, they are much alike: both are elegies cast in the dream form, following many of the conventions of the *Romance of the Rose* tradition.[17] Chaucer makes use of many of the same dream qualities used by the *Pearl*-poet, including the bemused dreamer and the dream transformation of a real person into a somewhat different form. But the effect is quite different. The two poems show the imprint of two quite different poets, and are no more alike than, say, *Hamlet* and *The Duchess of Malfi,* two works which are also of the same general period and genre (Elizabethan revenge tragedy) but essentially quite different.

The *Book of the Duchess* is much more closely related than *Pearl* to the courtly tradition, and the poetry of courtly love. It is, as many have commented, an imitative poem, incorporating lines, phrases, and situations from at least a half a dozen earlier dream visions.[18] It shows, however, a significant difference from the treatment of similar material by Chaucer's predecessors: like *Pearl,* it is not nearly so allegorical. Abstractions are almost completely absent as characters. The central action of the poem concerns human beings and a realistic predicament of human beings. Because of this minimizing of the allegorical element, C. S. Lewis feels that the poem loses any specifically dreamlike quality:

We dream in order to hear a bereaved lover give just such a literal account of his past happiness and present sorrow as he might have given in waking life. The dream is not, however, useless to Chaucer. It casts over his conversation with the lover a certain remoteness, it transfers the responsibility for what was said from his waking self to the vagaries of dream, and thus renders possible a more intimate picture of his patron's loss than would have been seemly on any other terms.[19]

[17]   Some scholars would protest that *Pearl*, since it is not a love poem but a religious vision, is *not* in the *Romance of the Rose* tradition; however, as noted above (p. 21), *Pearl* does have most of the earmarks of the genre, and many commentators have noted very specific resemblances to the *Romance of the Rose*, particularly ll. 749-753, on which Gordon comments in his introduction, p. xxxii. See also the note on these lines, p. 72. It is perhaps worth noting here that if this is the poet who wrote *Purity*, he definitely knew the *Romance*, and spoke approvingly of it as Clopyngnel's "clene Rose"; *Purity,* ed. Robert J. Menner (New Haven, 1920), p. 40.

[18]   Among writers who indicate various sources are Robinson, pp. 266 and 773; G. L. Kittredge, *Chaucer and His Poetry* (Cambridge, Mass., 1924), pp. 55-66; J. L. Lowes, *Geoffrey Chaucer* (Oxford, 1934), p. 101; Nevill Coghill, *The Poet Chaucer* (London, 1949), p. 22; and Haldeen Braddy, *Chaucer and the French Poet Graunson* (Baton Rouge, 1947), pp. 57-60.

[19]   *The Allegory of Love* (London, 1948), pp. 167-168.

But dreams very often do contain material that is just what we might encounter in waking life, or so it seems at the time. Other writers have maintained that the use of real individuals instead of allegorical figures makes this poem more, not less, like a real dream.[20] Then, too, the people in the dream are not exactly as they would be in waking life. Indisputably, the dream is more realistic than those in earlier poems of this tradition; but the realism is dream realism, not everyday, waking realism, and the whole structure of the poem is attuned to Chaucer's observation of how a dream works.

The dream is, like that of *Pearl,* psychologically motivated. The poet tells us, at the beginning, that he is in a state of misery, caused, he implies, by unrequited love.[21] Since, the poet tells us, he was unable to sleep because of his melancholy, he sat up late at night reading a book in which he found a story that fascinated him. The story was, of course, one about the sorrows of a person in love – what other subject would have interested a lovesick insomniac? This was the story of Seys and Alcyone, which he proceeds to relate in some detail.

Many critics have considered this Seys and Alcyone episode as "a serious breach of artistic unity," [22] a digression that is not an integral part of the poem.[23] The appropriateness of the reading matter to the presumed state of mind of the poet has been noted. It is even more appropriate to the dream that follows because the dream deals with precisely the same situation, the sorrow felt by the survivor upon the death of a loved one. But the story of Alcyone is about a bereaved woman, while in the dream that follows, a man is bereaved. The feeling of some critics seems to be that this is carelessness on Chaucer's part, that the two stories are not as well related as they might be. But the

[20] See, e.g., James R. Kreuzer, "The Dreamer in the *Book of the Duchess*", *PMLA*, LXVI (1951), pp. 543-547.

[21] This was a conventional way for a poet to begin his poem, and he expresses the idea in quite conventional terms. Even the statement of the precise number of years during which he has suffered is traceable to another poem, as Roger Sherman Loomis has demonstrated ("Chaucer's Eight Years Sickness", *MLN*, LIX [1944], pp. 178-180). But even if it is a convention, it is immediately apparent that it has some relevancy to the theme of the poem, the sorrow of a lover who has lost his beloved.

[22] Robert Kilburn Root, *The Poetry of Chaucer* (New York, 1950), p. 61.

[23] J. S. P. Tatlock considers that "Chaucer's version is less moving than Ovid's, one-sided, concerns only the wife's grief, and is less fitting to the rest of his poem, which is only of a bereaved husband's love ...." Furthermore, he ascribes to the episode a "gentle drowsy feeling and a simplemindedness"; *The Mind and Art of Chaucer* (Syracuse, N.Y., 1950), p. 27. Root (p. 61) dismisses the story as an "imitation of Ovid".

real difference between the two cases is simply that the man and the woman's roles are exchanged, and such a switch of identities, as any student of dream psychology knows, is highly characteristic of dreams. Furthermore, the change of emphasis here may be compared to the change of emphasis from the poet's waking thoughts of unrequited love to his reading about, and dreaming about, happy lovers whose sorrow is caused by the death of the beloved. It is the same subject – the sorrows of love – but from a different vantage point. Just as there is a parallel between the queen who grieved for her dead husband and the knight who grieved for his dead lady, so there is a parallel between the consolation that comes to the poet, enabling him to forget his own sorrows and go to sleep, through reading of the plight of a person to whom love brought a different kind of grief from his own, and the consolation offered, in a subtle way, in the dream to the bereaved knight, the consolation of being able to talk about his lost lady's perfections and the implication that he was fortunate to have had her love, if only for a short time. The Alcyone episode thus provides a psychological motivation for the dream, a connection between the dreamer's waking thoughts and his dream.[24]

The dream begins with a May morning, conventionally enough.[25] It might be somewhat far-fetched to try to make a case for the May morning as essentially true to dream psychology, but what follows in the dream has a definite connection. The dreamer sees depicted on the walls of his chamber various familiar stories of epic and romance, which might very naturally have been called to his mind by the circumstance that he has just been reading a similar story.[26] Further, the leader of the hunt that immediately materializes in a thoroughly

[24] It is also an integral part of the structure of the poem inasmuch as it provides parallels and balances that emphasize the parallels and balances of the rest of the poem. – Yet another function of the episode is remarked by Bertrand H. Bronson (*In Search of Chaucer* [Toronto, 1960], pp. 42-43: "It sheds the dignity of classical example, a poignant but statuesque and generalized beauty, muted with distance, over the shock and clamour of present anguish."

[25] But this "convention" is also useful to the structure of the poem. It may even be a realistic note as well: May may have been the proper time of the year for hunting the hart, as suggested by Oliver Farrar Emerson (*Chaucer Essays and Studies* [Cleveland, 1929] pp. 358-359). Kemp Malone (*Chapters on Chaucer* [Baltimore, 1951], p. 31) points out its usefulness as contrast, its joyful note contrasting with the misery of the Black Knight. It contrasts not only with what follows but also with what precedes; the poet's opening mood is hardly that of the merry May morning of his dreams.

[26] Cf. Skeat's note to line 333: "He likens the walls to the page of a book, in which the *glose*, or commentary, was often written on the margin."

dreamlike, illogical manner is said to be the "emperour Octovyen",
who is mentioned in various poems and romances, perhaps even in the
one the dreamer read just before going to sleep, if that was Machaut's
version of the Alcyone story.[27] Therefore, the hunt is connected, too,
with the dreamer's waking thoughts in a perfectly logical (for a dream)
series of connections.

There may be other reasons for the presence of "Octovyen" in the
poem. Ward thought it "probably a flattering allegory for the King",[28]
and Patch remarks: "Perhaps Octovyen is brought in ... as the em-
peror of the Golden Age, which, the poet thus implies, obtained during
the happy reign of Edward the Third. It is similarly that Deschamps
several times refers to him. 'Quant verray je le temps Octovien', he
asks, 'Que toute paix fut au monde affermée?' "[29] But even if this
implication was intended by the poet, it does not at all rule out the
previously stated reason for the use of this particular name for the
leader of the hunt. A figure in a dream may stand for two or three
different people; in fact, as we have noted, it is one of the better known
characteristics of dreams. There is nothing to prevent Octovyen from
simultaneously representing, by dream substitution, both King Edward
and John of Gaunt.[30]

The events that precede the appearance of the Knight in Black are
in perfect accord with the ways of a dream. The dreamer's horse van-
ishes as inexplicably as he appeared, and so does the celebrated puppy,
but all of this is taken for granted and does not cause any wonder on
the part of the dreamer. It seems perfectly natural to him, because he
is dreaming, and that is the way a dream works.

Perhaps this point provides a clue to the much-debated question of
the character of the dreamer. Tatlock stated: "Indifference to human
reality is most marked of all in the dreamer (who is in no sense Chaucer
himself)."[31] Kittredge similarly maintained that the dreamer is certainly
not Chaucer and definitely a simpleton, but he argued that this adds
to the dreamlike quality, saying that the *Book of the Duchess* "is really
like a dream. This effect, which every reader must instantly admit, is

[27] Cf. Lowes, p. 98.
[28] Adolphus William Ward, *Chaucer* (New York, 1880), p. 69.
[29] *On Rereading Chaucer* (Cambridge, Mass., 1948), pp. 199-200.
[30] Cf. Robinson's note, p. 775.
[31] *Mind and Art*, p. 30. He goes on to say that "perhaps such forgetfulness is
dreamlike," but does not speak with any great conviction, judging from such
remarks as "dreamer's bewildered apathy ... entirely unlike Chaucer's later
way ... here he makes a really inexplicable blur".

partly due to the naïveté of the Dreamer's temperament, which we contemplate, as we read, with something of that tolerant superiority with which we remember, in our waking moments, the innocent faith we have accorded to the irrationalities of dreamland . . ." [32]

Lowes,[33] Patch,[34] and Shelly,[35] among others, have agreed that the dreamer is a naive simpleton, not to be confused with Geoffrey Chaucer. But a number of writers in recent years have found the dreamer to be, on the contrary, tactful, courtly, and alert to all the finer points of courtly etiquette.[36] Even scholars who feel that the dreamer is wide awake and tactful have maintained that this does not mean that he represents Chaucer.[37] Yet, no one doubts that the dreamer, awake or asleep, of the other dream poems is Chaucer, even if a comic, modestly belittling portrait. And there is a relationship between the self- depreciating Chaucer of the later poems and this dreamer: Kittredge, the most eminent supporter of the theory that the dreamer cannot possibly be Chaucer, made this point, but he regarded the later dreamer as a new approach.[38]

It is undeniable that the dreamer is apparently forgetful and even tactless. A part of this characterization may well be attributed to Chaucer's ironic portrayal of himself; this could be taken as a sort of sketch for his later self-portraits. But there is a further possibility: the dreamer, whether or not Chaucer himself is intended, is somewhat confused and illogical because he is dreaming. It seems likely that Chaucer intended himself to be understood as the dreamer in view of the fact that his poems were "published" by being read aloud, presumably by Chaucer himself; so it would have been rather difficult for the audience not to understand "I" as the poet; but this interpretation

---

[32] *Chaucer and His Poetry*, p. 68; cf. pp. 48-51.

[33] Page 100.

[34] Pages 29, 33.

[35] Percy Van Dyke Shelly, *The Living Chaucer* (Philadelphia, 1940), pp. 48, 50.

[36] It has also been suggested that the dreamer is a doctrinaire, bookish adherent of courtly love, and that his seemingly unnecessary questions are asked in order to establish the exact circumstances that would affect the magnitude of the knight's loss, according to the code of courtly love; see John Lawlor, "The Pattern of Consolation in the *Book of the Duchess*", *Speculum*, XXXI (October, 1956), pp. 626-648.

[37] Kreuzer, pp. 543-547.

[38] *Op. cit.*, p. 76. – Coghill, however, does not think there is such a gulf between the two characterizations, and considers it Chaucer's first introduction of himself as a comic character: "a simpleton, a man of unsuccess but of excellent good will, an asker of foolish questions and not a great giver of wise answers" (p. 28).

would not mean that Chaucer was bound to present himself in a fully realistic light, as his comic pictures of himself elsewhere testify. The important thing is that he is relating a dream, and it is perfectly consistent with anyone's character that in a dream he should be absent-minded and just a little confused; it is also, of course, "consistent with medieval literary practice", as Birney remarked in a passage quoted above (p. 62); the dreamer of *Pearl* was also somewhat befuddled.[39]

There are other points of dream psychology in this poem, but we must be very careful not to go too far in reading in meanings which are not there. The poet's observation was obviously extraordinary, and some elements of the most modern kind of psychology are undoubtedly there. Bronson has pointed out the dreamer's identification with the Knight in Black, hinted at by verbal parallels in several passages.[40] He suggests that the dreamer's waking grief has been "renounced" in his dream "to reappear externalized and projected upon the figure of the grieving knight", with the result that "the knight's long and rapturous eulogy of his lost lady would serve, in the Dreamer's unconscious, to discharge the latter's sense of guilt for the disloyalty of wishing the death of that Merciles Beaute."[41]

This may seem to be going too far in the direction of Freudian psychology, but there is some undeniable truth in it. The parallelism between the situations of the dreamer, the story he reads, and the story he dreams has already been discussed, and it seems but a step further (and a very logical step) to see the mourning knight of the dream as a kind of projection of the dreamer's waking sorrows.[42] It is highly typical of the dream state that the situation preying on the dreamer's mind should be portrayed not exactly as it is but as something else combining other ideas and impressions: and in this case it

---

[39] It is even possible that the very specific indications of the vagaries of the dream state (e.g., the vanishing horse) occupy their positions in the poem to serve as a warning to the reader (or listener) that this is really a dream, that he must not expect the ensuing conversation to be bound by the kind of logic expected in waking life.

[40] Bertrand H. Bronson, "The *Book of the Duchess* Reopened", *PMLA*, LXVII (October, 1956), 871-872; also in *Chaucer: Modern Essays in Criticism*, ed. Edward Wagenknecht (New York, 1959), 281-283. The lines in question are: 18-21: 467-469; 25-26: 489-492; 6-7, 11-13: 509-511. Cf. also 39-40: 570.

[41] *Ibid.*, p. 871; in Wagenknecht, p. 281.

[42] Another parallelism is suggested by E. T. Donaldson in an essay on the *Book of the Duchess* (*Chaucer's Poetry* [New York, 1958], p. 953): "The Dreamer opens the heart of the grieving Knight with a naïve sympathy that is not unlike the little dog's."

combines his own situation with that of the bereaved wife he has just been reading of.

This parallelism, fusion, and inversion is not only sound dream psychology but also, of course, sound structural development. It exists in some forms outside of the dream itself; as Preston remarks, "the theme of sleep of the introduction is overturned when Chaucer's messenger approaches the god and blows a horn *ryght in here eere* . . ." [43]

Finally, when the poet awoke, he found in his hand the book he had been reading, "Of Alcione and Seys the king". He saw a connection between the story and the dream, indicating it to his readers in the clearest way possible.

The function of the dream in the *Book of the Duchess,* then, is basically twofold: it serves as an excuse and motivation and as a unifying structural device. The *Pearl*-poet had used it in the same way, but to totally different effect. The reasons for this seem clear: the purposes, themes, and moods of the two poems, although they are both elegies, are not at all related. One is a deeply serious discussion of a theological issue, as well as an expression of personal grief of the most poignant kind. The other is a tactful expression of sympathy for the grief of another, its purpose eulogy of the dead lady and consolation of her bereaved husband. Both the eulogy and the consolation are in purely human terms; Christian views of death and the afterlife are not so much as mentioned. In line with this humanistic orientation, Chaucer's use of dream psychology is not particularly symbolic, but much more "psychological", aiming at a realistic verisimilitude. This made his use of the *Romance of the Rose* echoes entirely different from the *Pearl*-poet's use. The garden surroundings, for example, which represent a genuinely unearthly paradise, theologically symbolic, in the religious context of *Pearl,* are here justified on the purely psychological level: the poet has been reading romances, and therefore dreams of a setting similar to that in his reading.

What these two poems have in common is not really their purpose, although they are both elegies; they are elegies with entirely different purposes. Nor is there any really striking similarity in the echoes of the older dream vision poems to be found in both. Their real affinity is as dream literature, poems which use the peculiar psychology of dreams as a help in achieving their particular aims.

[43]   Raymond Preston, *Chaucer* (London, 1952), pp. 37-38.

VI

CHAUCER'S FURTHER EXPERIMENTS WITH THE DREAM VISION

While Chaucer's use of the dream form in the *Book of the Duchess* showed many departures from the precedents set by earlier vision poems, these departures are mainly in the direction of psychological dream realism, in a literal way. His later dream visions seem almost to abandon this attempt, and yet in many ways they seem closer to "reality", less tied to the world of literary romance. The three poems – the *House of Fame*, the *Parliament of Fowls*, and the Prologue to the *Legend of Good Women* – are distinctly different from each other, and even more different from the *Book of the Duchess*, in mood, theme, and purpose (insofar as we can judge these matters in the first two cases), and Chaucer uses the dream as a helpful device to a different extent in each. But it is not just a matter of extent: the function of the dream appears to be essentially different in each case, and therefore the elements which can be called "dreamlike" are subtly different in each of the three later poems. Chaucer seems clearly to have been experimenting with the form, doing new and different things with it, in each case: but always using it in some significant fashion.

It is very difficult to identify the functions of the dream in the *House of Fame*, since the poem is, as we know it, incomplete; the tidings that do not quite come may have been of a nature that would affect our opinion and understanding of every other part of the poem.[1] But we must

---

[1] Most of the guesses regarding a possible ending have not helped matters much: if the poem was designed to announce a court engagement – that of Richard and Anne or any other – then the poet has certainly been guilty of writing a most disunified poem. Bronson ("Chaucer's *Hous of Fame*: Another Hypothesis", *Univ. of Calif. Publ. in Eng.*, III, iv [1934], 171-192) argues that we must suspect any theory that leads to a presumption of disunity, and points out the ridiculousness of this poem as an engagement present. (Cf. also Kittredge, p. 15: "*Chaucer always knew what he was about*".) Another conjecture is that Chaucer started out to write a conventional medieval love-vision but was carried so far afield by his classical material that he found it impossible to get back to the original plan and therefore never tried to finish the poem; Edgar Finlay

look at what is there, rather than bemoan what is missing, and what is there is clearly stated to be a dream. Chaucer begins the poem with the passage on dreams already discussed.[2] In this passage he shows considerable doubt about the accepted theories of dream interpretation, handling the whole thing in a humorous vein. He gives no clues to the type of dream we are to expect, or what could have caused the dream – logically enough: he is explaining that he cannot tell what causes dreams, and is dubious about their classification. He would only be contradicting himself if he proceeded to make the cause and type of this dream evident.[3] This is fair warning that we cannot expect the same kind of dream psychology found in the *Book of the Duchess*. But it is also a very elaborate way of calling attention to the fact that what follows is a dream: and the fact that it is very definitely a dream must have some significance. Chaucer would not have made such a point of it if he had not intended to use it.

One theory is that the dream is here merely a convention. Malone, after noting the presence of characteristic dream psychology in the *Book of the Duchess*, says: "Nothing of the kind appears in the *House of Fame*, where the dream is used, conventionally enough, as a vehicle for wonders impossible in actual life."[4] A slightly more dreamlike quality is allowed by Tatlock, who feels that the dream form here "gives lifelike freedom for rambling and inconsequence, more notable in this poem than elsewhere in Chaucer".[5] But this qualification is

---

Shannon, *Chaucer and the Roman Poets* (Cambridge, Mass., 1929), pp. 117-118. Another idea is that the man of great authority may be there to tell not one tiding but many; this explanation is more plausible, in spite of the fact that this is a "lytel laste bok", for it could be possible that the man of great authority might be a fellow poet – Dante, for example – who would not necessarily have to tell all the tidings then and there. Cf. Robert J. Allen, "A Recurring Motif in Chaucer's *House of Fame*", *JEGP*, LV (July, 1956), 403; Paul G. Ruggiers, "The Unity of Chaucer's *House of Fame*", *SP*, L (1953), 16-29; also in *Chaucer: Modern Essays in Criticism*, ed. Edward Wagenknecht (New York, 1959), pp. 295-308.

[2] See p. 34.

[3] Curry states (*Chaucer and the Medieval Sciences* [New York, 1926], p. 238) that this is "pure *somnium coeleste*" and that the poet therefore forfeits the privilege of using the psychology of the *somnium animale*. However, the poet has gone to such pains to state that the dream cannot be classified that this seems an unwarranted assumption.

[4] *Chapters on Chaucer* (Baltimore, 1951), p. 49. It is then natural that he thinks the introductory portion "has no organic connection with the dream" (p. 47).

[5] J. S. P. Tatlock, *The Mind and Art of Chaucer* (Syracuse, New York, 1950), p. 56.

dangerous, implying a disorganization and lack of plan to the poem.

Lowes, however, has made a good case for dream psychology in the poem in a literary sense: "But his mind ... is really playing, as in a dream, with recollections of his reading in the *romances*, and weaving from them a fabric like which neither Benoit, nor he who wrote the *Thebaid*, nor the maker of *Li Hystore de Julius Cesar* ever dreamed." [6] Patch has pointed out a good example of this kind of association:

But since Fame's abode according to Ovid was on a mountain Chaucer would be reminded of the strange journey to Fortune's house on a rocky height in the *Anticlaudianus* of Alain de L'Isle, and that in turn would recall the flight with birds to Fortune's house on the rock of ice in the *Panthere d'Amours* of Nicole de Margival. ... The dreamer in Nicole de Margival's poem visited Venus and then found himself in a desolate region, from which the story leads on to the scene of Fortune's lofty abode. [7]

This kind of literary association, common in medieval poetry, could be dismissed as insignificant, except for the fact that it is typical of the dreaming mind, and therefore provides some slight indication of dream psychology. Interestingly enough, it does suggest dream psychology here, even if it was a matter of common practice, since this treatment is typical of Chaucer's use of the conventions.

The interplay of literary associations, and a rather unexpected logic by which they are connected with each other and with the ideas they evoke, seem to me to provide the structural basis of this poem. While we will probably never know what the final tidings were to be, there is a traceable chain of thought in the poem up to this point. For reasons he playfully but specifically declines to speculate upon, the poet dreams he is in a temple of Venus. This situation apparently reminds him of Venus' son, Aeneas, and he sees the story of Aeneas painted on the wall. Prominent in this story is the desertion of Dido, and in this connection the subject of "fame" is first introduced in a context far from favorable. It is "wikke Fame" that concerns Dido, the loss of her good reputation as a result of her love affair with Aeneas. [8] This leads the dreaming poet to think of other cases in which a love affair has led to disaster. He is then carried off by the eagle to hear some fresher tidings, which, it is suggested, will confirm his impression of the unreliability of love's pleasures. The house of Fame, where such things would naturally be known, provides an example of the unreliability of another (but connected) human desideratum, affording an opportunity

---

[6] *Geoffrey Chaucer* (Oxford, 1934), p. 112.
[7] *On Rereading Chaucer* (Cambridge, Mass., 1948), pp. 40-41.
[8] Lines 300-360.

for him to hear a group of people in every way unworthy accorded the fame of great lovers.[9] Ready to hear some sort of news, he proceeds to the central gathering place for all tidings, false as well as true. This news, it would follow, will probably not be the polite tidings of true love so necessary if the poet were celebrating a court engagement: such tidings would destroy the continuity of the entire poem. On the other hand, it is equally unlikely that the news will be tragic, for the whole tone of the poem, from the introductory passage about dreams, is one of light and mocking humor. Chaucer's news, therefore, would probably show "love" in a rather unfavorable light, almost certainly as of a somewhat humorous nature. Bronson argues that the "Fame" to be announced will probably be "bad eminence", not "good".[10] As he cogently demonstrates, the internal evidence is overwhelmingly in favor of tidings of this nature.

This continuity shows not only a unified structure for the poem, but also a series of associations that could very well be good dream psychology. Nothing here, however, is definitely the province of the dreaming mind alone, a fact that harmonizes with the Proem to the poem. Because the poet has deliberately made the dream ambiguous, his audience can maintain that it is several different types, but cannot narrow it down to any one variety.

It is worth noting that many of the details of the dreamer's experience are simultaneously true to dream experience and right in line with literary convention. The vision of figures painted on the wall – in this case, of course, the story of the Aeneid – is a commonplace; there is a certain amount of dialogue as Chaucer tells the story, but in the main it is something seen on a wall, and so vividly portrayed that the dreamer is frightened by the painted storm. It is thus dreamlike in that it is something visualized, but a scene which will not stay put in its original terms (i.e., a flat and lifeless painting), that tends to take on a life of its own. Then, after seeing the sights of the temple, Chaucer goes out and finds himself in a deserted region, by no means to his

---

[9] Then, too, according to the conventions of courtly love, love was the basis of all good courtly behavior, and it is to be presumed that anyone worthy of good fame would have to meet the requirement of being a proper courtly lover. The variation between Fame's suitors, good and bad, and the totally unfair treatment they receive is also related to the theme of love as treated in the two preceding "books", in that it shows another aspect of the unreliability of such human goals as love and fame.

[10] "Chaucer's Hous of Fame", pp. 184-187, and *In Search of Chaucer* (Toronto, 1960), pp. 39-40.

liking. Conventional as this may be, it also has some truth as a familiar dream situation.

The dream qualities of the *House of Fame* are elusive; but so is every other aspect of this delightful and puzzling poem. I have attempted to indicate factors which seem to me to be in some sense significant here; I do not wish to drive them into the ground. It is ironic – but true – that the way in which this poem most resembles a dream is in its refusal to be pinned down.

It seems evident that while Chaucer is again using the dream as a unifying device, he is not treating it very seriously in this poem. His playful preliminary discussion makes this clear. He does not attempt to make the dream confirm to recognizable dream situations, such as the disappearing puppy of the *Book of the Duchess,* except in the rather sketchy ways indicated above. He is not really trying to convince anyone that this dream could have happened: he is writing a basically humorous poem, as the second book should certainly make clear to any reader who is confused by the opening sections. He is presenting himself not simply as a "daswed" dreamer (although he certainly is that), but also as a downright comic character. Here the dream is, then, largely an excuse for fantastic situations; but it is not to be thought of as *solely* an excuse. Chaucer makes a simple, if subtle, use of the fact that these things purport to have happened in a dream, including the unifying function discussed above.

The dream also appears to be used for unification in the *Parliament of Fowls.* While this poem, unlike the *House of Fame,* is a complete poem, the problems in understanding it appear to be quite similar. A good deal of debate on its occasion, its meaning, and its unity, or lack of it, has arisen. For a large variety of reasons, the more recent critics of the poem have tended to discard the search for a personal, allegorical interpretation and to defend the unity of the poem. A good part of this unity can be attributed to the fact that the poem is a dream, and follows, like Chaucer's other dream visions, a specific dream logic. This poem, like the others, has an introductory portion of considerable length before the actual dream begins; and, as in the *Book of the Duchess* and the *House of Fame,* some commentators have found it difficult to understand the connection between the introduction and the dream proper. But here again there is a definite connection, and the poem surely cannot be correctly understood as a whole unless we give careful attention to the preliminary sections.

Chaucer begins with two stanzas expressing considerable puzzlement over this business of "love", which is officially his concern as a court poet, "al be that I knowe nat Love in dede".[11] Then, in reading, searching for better answers to his questions, Chaucer tells us that he came across "Tullyus of the Drem of Scipioun", which is, of course, contained within the commentary of our old friend Macrobius.[12] The poet says he was so absorbed in this book that he read it all day, not even noticing the passage of time, and he proceeds to summarize it. But, he says finally that he was not satisfied with what he had learned:

> For bothe I hadde thyng which that I nolde,
> And ek I nadde that thyng that I wolde.[13]

He had not found a satisfactory answer to his questions on the meaning of it all, and what he had found did not seem to bear on the power of "love".[14]

At this point comes the adaptation from Claudian discussed above,[15] and while Chaucer is careful to say he really is not sure that this reading was the cause of his dream, the implication is clear. Just as his reading of the story of Alcyone, together with his presumed personal interest in its theme of the sorrows of love, led him to dream of a similar situation, his reading of the dream of Scipio now has led him to dream that he, too, was conducted to a sort of heaven by Scipio Africanus.[16] But it is a heaven with a difference.

[11]   Line 8.
[12]   As the poet points out below in l. 111.
[13]   Lines 90-91.
[14]   R. M. Lumiansky ("Chaucer's *Parliament of Foules*: a Philosophical Interpretation", *RES*, XXIV [1948], 81-89) feels that what the poet is searching is a personal thing: a way to reconcile his status as a poet of love with his knowledge of the vanity of courtly love. This interpretation is possible, of course, but it seems to me overly personal. Chaucer so rarely takes himself seriously in his poetry that it seems a more impersonal explanation would be preferable. Actually, Chaucer is likely to go out of his way *not* to reveal his personal feelings directly. Cf. also Bronson, "In Appreciation of Chaucer's Parlement of Foules", *Univ. of Calif. Publ. in Eng.*, III (1935), 193 ff.
[15]   See p. 35.
[16]   Although this recalls the opening remarks about Macrobius in the *Romance of the Rose*, the book as motivation for the dream is probably Chaucer's own contribution to the dream vision tradition. Sypherd and Robinson both mention the device of telling about the book the poet had been reading when he fell asleep as a common one. However, Marshall Stearns has pointed out that the book as motivation is almost non-existent before Chaucer's time, the only other possible source being Froissart, in "L'Espinette Amoureuse", and that it became popular after Chaucer used it to such good effect, rather than vice-versa. See W. O. Sypherd, *Studies in Chaucer's 'House of Fame'* (London, 1907), p. 10; Robinson, p. 315; and Marshall W. Stearns, "Chaucer Mentions a Book", *MLN*, LVII (1942), 28-31.

The difference between the moral universe of the *Somnium Scipionis* and the garden of love Chaucer describes has led many critics to the conclusion that there is no true connection between the introduction and the dream. Goffin points out that Chaucer's garden is closely related to the earthly one of the *Romance of the Rose,* suggesting that the connection between this garden and that of Scipio Africanus is merely the fact that Macrobius is mentioned at the beginning of the *Romance.*[17] Tatlock considers the entire Scipio sequence completely irrelevant, catering to the medieval taste for classical references *per se.*[18] Root finds the sequence "creaky machinery".[19] Bronson also finds it incongruous, but he attributes it to the "topsy-turvey logic of dreams".[20] It is possible that all these critics are to some degree correct: it is perfectly good dream logic that Scipio would show Chaucer an entirely different kind of paradise because Chaucer's interest was connected with, but not the same as, the philosophy he found interesting in the story; it is indeed machinery, since the story provides the occasion of the dream. That Chaucer and his audience would have liked it all the better for being a classical reference is undeniable; and the tenuous connection between Macrobius and the garden of the Rose is another bit of valid dream psychology, indicative of Chaucer's careful attention to detail.

Chaucer's Scipio does not, then, take him up among the stars (as the eagle did in the *House of Fame*), but to a garden that contains echoes of three of Chaucer's favorite authors: Guillaume de Lorris, Boccaccio, and Dante.[21] It is no doubt part of the humor that the garden so reminiscent of the *Romance of the Rose* – and dozens of other poems in the same tradition – should be entered through Dantean gates, but it is probably a private joke, as Patch points out.[22] Perhaps it also has significance as dream psychology: one particular book has

[17]   R. C. Goffin, "Heaven and Earth in the 'Parlement of Foules'", *MLR*, XXXI (1936), pp. 493-499.
[18]   *Mind and Art*, pp. 65-70.
[19]   *The Poetry of Chaucer* (New York, 1950) p. 66.
[20]   "In Appreciation of Chaucer's Parlement of Foules", p. 203.
[21]   This is not to say that the garden may not also suggest a good deal more. As J. A. W. Bennett remarks, such gardens in medieval art and literature have many implications: civilization itself, art, Eden, Tir na n-og, etc. See *The Parlement of Foules: an Interpretation* (Oxford, 1957), pp. 62-63.
[22]   *Op. cit.,* pp. 46-47. Cf. also pp. 44-45. This kind of private significance should be a familiar story to readers today, since poets of our own time seem particularly given to it.

motivated this dream, but, as is typical of dreams, it becomes confused with several others in the dream.

Chaucer the dreamer is just as bemused as he was in the *House of Fame*, and his guide speaks to him with the same patronizing note that the eagle used. And then this guide disappears into thin air: after he takes Chaucer's hand in his and leads him into the garden, he is no longer necessary, and, without a word of farewell or any notice that he dropped Chaucer's hand, he is heard from no more. This disappearance, similar to the vanishing of the puppy and the horse in the *Book of the Duchess,* serves the same purpose: it happens just as it would in a dream.[23] There is, moreover, a very good reason why the dreamer no longer needs his support – Chaucer, as the dreamer, would have felt very much at home in the garden that he has now entered.

This is a literary garden, familiar to all readers of dream vision poems. The dreaming poet recognized it the instant he entered the gates, for he noted that the trees were covered with leaves "that ay shal laste".[24] All the details that follow are familiar: the catalogued trees, the river in the green meadow, the flowers, the birds, the carefully selected beasts, the even climate, and the well. Even the eternal daylight is reminiscent of the garden of the Rose.[25] As is inevitable in this garden, he sees Cupid and his arrows, and a host of abstractions.

But some of the abstractions the poet notes are not entirely pleasant in their connotations: Foolhardiness and Flattery, for example, and

> the Craft that can and hath the myght
> To don by force a wyght to don folye –
> Disfigurat was she, I nyl nat lye.[26]

And then he comes to the temple, where all is not quite as it should be. Many of the votaries, he plainly states (l. 234), were not "fayre of hemself", but simply "gay". A moving spirit in this temple is Jealousy, hardly one of the more pleasant aspects of love. Venus herself does not fare too well, as compared with her description in Chaucer's "source", Boccaccio:

---

[23] As Professor Helaine Newstead has remarked to me, this is also similar to the disappearance of Virgil in Dante's *Commedia*.

[24] Line 173.

[25] *Roman de la Rose*, ed. Ernest Langlois (Paris, 1912), V, 48, ll. 20559-20562:
> Cist la nuit en essil enveie,
> Cist fait le jour qua dit avaie,
> Qui dure pardurablement,
> Senz fin e senz comencement.

[26] Lines 220-222.

> Ma avie d'oro i crini e rilucenti
> Intorno al capo sanza treccia alcuna:
> Il suo viso era tal che le piú genti
> Hanno a rispetto bellezza nissuna:
> Le braccia, il petto e la poma eminenti
> Si vedien tutte, e ogni altri parte d'una
> Testa tanto sottil si ricopria,
> Che quasimente nuda comparia.[27]

This, at Chaucer's hands, becomes:

> Hyre gilte heres with a golden thred
> Ibounden were, untressed as she lay,
> And naked from the brest unto the hed
> Men myghte hire sen; and sothly for to say,
> The remenaunt was wel kevered to my pay,
> Ryght with a subtyl coverchef of Valence –
> Ther nas no thikkere cloth of no defense.[28]

Incidentally, Chaucer seems here to have forgotten that in the garden "ne nevere wolde it nyghte,/ But ay cler day to any manes syghte",[29] for his Venus is resting "Til that the hote sonne gan to weste." [30] It is quite possible that the poet was deliberately inconsistent, since the dream psychology is sound.

A pair of lovers are petitioning Venus for her help. Other lovers, famous lovers of antiquity, are portrayed on the walls of the temple, none of them happy in their love, as Chaucer points out:

> Alle these were peynted on that other syde,
> And al here love, and in what plyt they dyde.[31]

And, as Lowes remarked, Chaucer has added to Boccaccio's list lovers seen by Dante in the circle of carnal sinners.[32]

This garden of Venus, or love, is, then, a familiar tune – but played in a different key. Everything about it is conventional, but not quite flattering. It is entirely in keeping with Chaucer's earlier statements and mood, and it serves admirably as a contrast to the next phase of the dream, the birds that gather around Nature to choose their mates.

---

[27] *Teseide* VII, 65; in Skeat, *Complete Works of Geoffrey Chaucer* (Oxford, 1899), I, 73. Cf. Bronson, "In Appreciation of Chaucer's Parlement of Foules", pp. 209-211, and Lumiansky, p. 87 ff. Lumiansky considers the attitude toward Venus unfavorable because Venus has raised false hopes by sending the dream to the poet, presumably to show him an answer to his question, which it did not do.

[28] Lines 267-273.

[29] Lines 209-210.

[30] Line 266.

[31] Lines 293-294.

[32] Lowes, "Chaucer and Dante", *MP*, XIV (1916-17), pp. 705-735.

If the scenes in and around the temple of Venus portray a garden of courtly, or romantic, love, the remainder of the poem is definitely talking about natural love, no less so because the courtly variety is introduced in a humorous vein through the debate over the "hand" of the blushing formel. It may be that the birds represented historical figures (although that interpretation seems unlikely, since the setting is not one calculated to flatter the ego of a royal lover),[33] or that Chaucer was here satirizing the Valentine tradition,[34] or even alluding playfully to the Good Parliament of 1376,[35] or introducing an element of social satire.[36] But none of these things, which may or may not be elements in the poet's thinking, is really essential to the understanding of the poem, which is about love: love for our fellow man, the "commune profyt" expressed through Scipio; romantic, courtly love, which, he seems to imply, may have more penalties than rewards; and natural love between the sexes, leading to such a natural outcome as the mating of the birds. This doet not necessarily imply a matter of choice and contrast between these various "types" of love; they all exist as part of a whole.[37]

Miss Everett said of this poem: "This, then, is how I think the poem as a whole should be interpreted: as delicately ironical fantasy on the theme of love and not merely of Courtly Love presented through a series of contrasts, variously achieved." [38] It is, it seems, this technique of showing by contrasts, a technique used frequently by Chaucer, which misleads many readers into thinking the poem lacks unity. But this contrast within a unified theme is actually masterly construction; it is, as well, the best possible construction for a dream poem. Seeming inconsistencies, which prove, upon investigation, to be well connected, are the very essence of dream psychology.

Finally, we are again reminded that this is a dream, a very dream-like dream. Chaucer is awakened by the noise of the birds, just as the striking of a bell awoke him in the *Book of the Duchess*. As Kittredge

---

[33] Cf., e.g., Haldeen Braddy, "The *Parlement of Foules* In Its Relation to Contemporary Events", *Three Chaucer Studies* (New York, 1932).
[34] Gardiner Stillwell, "Unity and Comedy in Chaucer's Parlement of Foules", *JEGP*, XLIX (1950), p. 492; cf. C. S. Lewis, *The Allegory of Love* (London, 1938), pp. 171-176.
[35] Braddy, p. 84.
[36] Stillwell, esp. pp. 473-474.
[37] Cf. E. Talbot Donaldson, ed., *Chaucer's Poetry* (New York, 1958), p. 956.
[38] Dorothy Everett, *Essays on Middle English Literature*, ed. Patricia Kean (Oxford, 1955), p. 113.

said, "In both, the vision is finished, and the fancied abruptness is merely the instantaneous passage from sleep to waking." [39]

Chaucer's handling of dream psychology in the *Parliament of Fowls* bears many resemblances to his usage in both the *Book of the Duchess* and the *House of Fame*; here he has used some of the sort of psychology he used in the former, and some of the satirical, humorous overtones of the latter, both in one poem, the combination achieving a third and again quite different effect. The motivation and dream actions are analogous to those of the *Book of the Duchess,* but, as in the *House of Fame,* they are much more elusive. Chaucer has refused to be pinned down to a presumably realistic discussion of a "real" dream. Just as he did in the *House of Fame,* he refuses specifically to take himself or the dream quite seriously; he makes fun of himself as a bumbling, foolish character, not just a confused dreamer, and he questions the causes and credentials of the dream itself. The result seems to be that he is more than ever in control of the situation. He uses the dream for whatever it can give him, but does not let it dictate the content of the poem. He needs dream logic as a sort of glue to hold together the many facets of his poem, and to remind us that it is a dream he works in various aspects of dream psychology from time to time. But the dream is also, as in the *House of Fame,* an excuse for phantasy, and phantasy which has, at least, humorous overtones, although it also deals with serious, philosophical questions. The *Parliament of Fowls* is more serious than the *House of Fame,* and more philosophical and abstract than the *Book of the Duchess.* It called for a slightly different manipulation of the dream framework than that used in either of the previous poems.

Chaucer's last dream vision, the Prologue to the *Legend of Good Women*, bears various resemblances to the earlier poems, but it is again quite a different story. It is important to remember that this is not meant to be really complete in itself. It was written for a definite purpose, which was, as far as we can tell, a very different purpose from that of any other dream poem. This is a prologue, explaining how the poet came to write the group of non-dream stories that follow. It does not necessarily represent a complete point of view, an investigation of a question; it is an introduction to a group of poems, setting the unifying theme of the group.

Nevertheless, it is, of course, a dream vision poem, a unit in itself, and its structure, like that of Chaucer's other dream poems, shows

[39] *Chaucer and His Poetry* (Cambridge, Mass., 1924), pp. 22-23.

careful attention to the ways of dreams. The pattern is the same, generally, as that used in the other three dream poems: a preliminary statement suggesting that the poet is, or was, concerned with a particular train of thought is followed by remarks about his reading. We can infer that the two are connected. Either his reading has brought the thought to his mind, as is probably the case in the *House of Fame*, or the interest has dictated the choice of reading matter, as in the *Book of the Duchess*. This association reminds him of something, here of an interest that can tear him away, presumably, from his books, and he describes the exact events that occurred before he went to sleep and began to dream. The dream is, as usual, connected with his waking thoughts and activities. In it he meets figures who are easily identified with these waking preoccupations. When the dream reaches its climax, he awakes, abruptly, and proceeds to write.[40]

Not only is the pattern familiar; so are the problems. Among the questions about the poem that have been hotly debated are the occasion of the poem, or lack of one; the possible identification of its figures with actual people; whether or not Chaucer is serious in his praises of love. In this case these questions are of particular interest, since there is a clear indication that the poet is, to some extent, describing real events in his explanation of his choice of subject. It seems likely that the Queen was involved, as a great many readers have concluded from what appears to be a dedication to her in ll. 496-497. This reference has led many readers to think that it indicates a connection between Alceste, the dream figure who speaks the lines, and Queen Anne herself, a connection perfectly consistent with courtly protocol. After all it would not have been suitable or respectful for the bourgeois Chaucer to portray the Queen directly in his poem, for reasons similar to those that led him to disguise slightly the identity of John of Gaunt and Blanche of Lancaster in the *Book of the Duchess*.

But there may be other reasons besides propriety for the fact that the circumstances of the lady of the dream do not parallel those of the real queen. This is a dream, and the figure of Alceste can legitimately represent two or more individuals or ideas simultaneously. Chaucer's preliminary remarks concern the existence of heaven and hell and the scarcity of returned travellers to vouch for their reality. He states that he has been reading many "olde bokes" to learn more; we may infer that in these old books he could have found the story of one traveller

---

[40] At least, in 'G' he wakes up.

who did return, Alceste. Further, he speaks of his enjoyment of the spring, particularly of the daisy, which he spent the day admiring just before he had this particular dream. Therefore, it is quite consistent that when he fell asleep he dreamt of a lady who is both Alceste and the daisy; she could also be Anne of Bohemia.[41] A dream figure is not limited by daytime logic, as, even without benefit of Freud, Chaucer would not have failed to observe.

But the fact that Alceste is firmly identified with the daisy has led some commentators to contend that she therefore cannot be Queen Anne, on the grounds that the terms in which Chaucer expressed his admiration for the daisy were entirely too fervent to have been addressed to the queen of England. This opinion has led to a quest for an actual "sovreign lady", with the idea that Chaucer is expressing his own love for this elusive lady.[42] In view of Chaucer's detached − if not downright critical − attitude toward courtly love elsewhere in his poetry, it would seem highly unlikely that he is here seriously presenting himself as a courtly lover. Furthermore, there are reasons to think that his praises of the daisy are not necessarily expressions of strong personal feeling.

For one thing, it has been demonstrated again and again that the passage on the daisy is highly conventional, borrowing from a whole school of poetry: Robinson call it (p. 480) "almost a cento of quotations or imitations of contemporary poety, French and perhaps Italian". And there is the further probability that the poet is being somewhat ironic. The conventional enthusiasm is punctuated by typical Chaucerian self-depreciation, with obviously humorous intent, and also by references to quarrels between the flower and the leaf, which must refer to a debate or game going on at the court at the time, the details of which, unfortunately, have not come down to us. Chaucer's elaborate statements of his own impartiality on this question are linked to his remarks about his inability to compose poetry, a detail which throws a humorous light on this question (whatever it was), and, in turn, it is

---

[41] For *pro* arguments, see Tatlock, pp. 102-120, and Root, p. 142. Definitely *con* are Lowes, "The Prologue to the *Legend of Good Women* as Related to the French *Marguerite* Poems and the *Filostrato*", *PMLA*, XIX (1904), 593-683; Victor Langhans, "Zu Chaucers Traumgedichten und deren Auffassung durch A. Brusendorff", *Anglia*, LI (1927), 323-353; and Bronson, *In Search of Chaucer*, pp. 54-55.

[42] See, e.g., Margaret Galway, "The 'Troilus' Frontispiece", *MLR*, XLIV (1949), pp. 173-174, and Frederick Tupper, "Chaucer's Lady of the Daisies", *JEGP*, XXI (1922), pp. 293-317.

quite possible that the entire daisy passage is to be taken in an equally light spirit.[43]

Evidence that this may be the correct way to read the passage is found in the somewhat ironic treatment of the God of Love in the dream that follows. This portrayal of the "god" is similar to that in a dozen other dream poems – it is even somewhat exaggerated: Chaucer has heightened the pseudo-Christian atmosphere by adding a halo to the characteristics of the God of Love.[44] But this "god" does not ring true; he does not really know what he is talking about. His condemnation of the *Romance of the Rose* does not take into account the portion by Guillaume de Lorris, and, as Coghill remarks, at least two of the authors he cites as proper models were actually satirists on women.[45] There is perhaps also irony in the fact that the story of Medea, one of the "saints," comes from Jean de Meun's portion of the *Romance of the Rose*, as Preston has suggested.[46]

Certainly Chaucer's picture of himself in the dream is, as usual, comic. He is, once more, a bemused dreamer, being informed at great length of his shortcomings as a poet ("Al be hit that he kan nat wel endite"!) and of his ignorance in general. But all of this is presented with due respect to Alceste and the God of Love, whose orders he proceeds to follow.

If, then, this poem was dedicated to the queen, written on the occasion of some sort of protest at the unflattering reflections on womankind found in Criseyde, and, while utterly conventional in situation,[47] slightly mocking in its treatment of the conventions, it should not be taken too seriously. It is a playful poem, gently spoofing both the poet and the conventions of courtly love poetry, but only gently, for it also

---

[43] See, e.g., F, 69-83, 102; G, 61-78; F, 188-194.

[44] Cf. William Allen Neilson, *The Origins and Sources of the "Court of Love"* (Boston, 1899), p. 145: "This is the first passage in which I have seen the God of Love wearing a halo."

[45] *The Poet Chaucer* (London, 1949), p. 100. "Valerye" is probably Walter Map's *Epistola Valerii ad Rufinum ne uxorem ducat*, containing the story of the man who told a friend, weeping, that three of his wives had hanged themselves on a certain tree in his garden, whereupon the friend begged for a cutting.

[46] *Chaucer* (London, 1952), p. 129, n. 3. Germaine Dempster (*Dramatic Irony in Chaucer* [Stanford University, Calif., 1932], p. 338) states that the dream visions completely lack dramatic irony. Perhaps by the strictest definition of *dramatic* irony they do; but they certainly do not lack irony in other ways.

[47] Cf. Deschamps' *Le Lay Amoureux*, in which the poet lies hidden by a bush as he watches the God of Love and his court of famous historical and legendary lovers and allegorical personages, afraid to show himself; when he is discovered, he is defended by Love's folk as being one who has written well in the proper cause. – Cf. Neilson, pp. 76-77.

had to pay the poet's compliments to his queen and to the ladies of her court. It is perhaps part of the joke that it is all a dream: the poet cannot be held responsible, after all, for the vagaries of a mere dream!

In view of the wide differences between his four dream poems, it becomes obvious that Chaucer neither accepted nor rejected the conventions of dream vision poetry: he used them. Writing about courtly love in a courtly mode, he is neither an adherent to the code of courtly love nor a satirist attempt to expose its evils; neither an idealist nor a cynic. As Dodd remarks of his attitude toward courtly love, it is even unfair to say he is critical.[48] He does not condone error, but he does not condemn those who err or attempt "al croked to redresse".[49] He is detached, even from himself. This quality was peculiarly appropriate for his dream poems, where, dreamlike, points of view and individualities may fuse, the truth emerging from what appears at first glance to make little sense.[50]

Chaucer certainly intended his dreams to be recognizable in terms of universal human experience. He was primarily an observer of life, never a romantic, and in his use of a poetic form, which had previously been handled in a highly romantic fashion, he applied the touchstone of reality. He found the dream not a device, but a legitimate and sound poetic vehicle. To Chaucer, the dream was primarily a structural framework. Its other uses seem to be always secondary in his dream poems. Yet, he was quite aware of the variety of possibilities inherent in the dream, and he exploits various different aspects of dream psychology and philosophy as they seem appropriate – or useful – to him in four quite different poems.

[48] William George Dodd, *Courtly Love in Chaucer and Gower* (Boston, 1913), p. 253.
[49] *Balade de Bon Conseyl*, l. 8. R. S. Loomis ("Was Chaucer a Laodicean?" *Essays and Studies in Honor of Carleton Brown* [New York, 1940], pp. 129-148) argues that Chaucer's detachment was simply a politic and common-sense one, not complete, and suggests that this *Balade* summarizes his philosophy very neatly.
[50] Cf. Preston, p. 65: "Chaucer has his own way of examining a question: he will look at them one by one, so that he can think of them all together. It is not merely that ... Chaucer tells a story with different layers. He tells it ... from different points of view."

VII

DREAMING IN *PIERS PLOWMAN*

Piers Plowman is in every way a far cry from the finished neatness of *Pearl* and the sophisticated subtleties of Chaucer's visions. This huge, sprawling poem could not be confined to a single dream; its train of thought is in a sense continuous, but the ingredients are separate. Like *Pearl*, it is a serious, religious poem; like the *Parliament of Fowls*, it contains a good deal of humor and satire; like all the poems discussed above, it is a dream vision; but it is impossible to push the resemblances much further. For one thing, it is allegorical throughout. *Pearl* contains plenty of allegory;[1] but *Pearl* is not *an* allegory, any more than the *Book of the Duchess* is. Chaucer's dream poems contain personifications, such as Fame, and symbols verging on what is usually termed allegorical, such as the Daisy-Anne-Alceste figure of the Prologue to the *Legend of Good Women*; but few people today would maintain that any one of Chaucer's dream visions, is as a whole, allegorical. *Piers Plowman* is an allegory; or, if you will, a series of connected allegories. This fact alone means that the poet had to make quite different uses of the dream background in this poem.

Another significant difference between *Piers Plowman* and Chaucer's dream visions is, obviously, form. The fact that *Piers Plowman* is written in alliterative staves may or may not be of significance from the point of view of the poet's use of dream: it is almost impossible to be sure. In discussing Chaucer's use of suggestions of the actual dream state, I have purposely refrained from attempting to identify any specifically verbal elements, such as were notable in *Pearl*, for two reasons. The poetic forms Chaucer used in his visions were not so suggestive in this way in themselves as the form chosen by the

---

[1] Or symbolism, if it seems preferable to limit the word "allegory" to "describe a work or art as a whole (as *pastoral* is)", as Paul Pickrel has suggested; *Religious Allegory in Medieval England: an Introductory Study Based on the Vernacular Sermon Before 1250*, unpub. diss. (Yale, 1944), p. 10.

Pearl-poet, and the puns and word play to be found in Chaucer's work are just as frequent – if not more so – in his non-dream poetry. It would therefore seem dangerous to try to attach any specific intention of conveying a dream atmosphere to the use of word play in Chaucer. It seems rather probable that this aspect of dream psychology simply did not occur to him. The case of *Piers Plowman* is something else again. There is a definite, noticeable element of verbal echoing, of using one word with several meanings or several words which sound alike but are not the same. A good example of ambiguous or punning wording is "glose" as used in B. Prol. 60; also, "borghe", II, 87, and "metelees", VII. 141.[2] Words which sound similar include "*lewed* men *leued* hym wel" (italics added), Prol. 72, and "Mede the mayde", as in II. 20. But this sort of thing is almost inevitable when we are dealing with alliterative poetry – it is part of the verse form. And, in this case, the verse form is absolutely traditional and conventional; one can scarcely maintain that the poet chose it because of its possibilities in echoing dream-use of language. Still, the element is there to a striking extent, and it is not impossible that the poet may have considered its appropriateness.

While Langland's choice of words may or may not be deliberately ambiguous, there is no doubt that his use of them is often terribly ambiguous, and, consequently, dreamlike. Although it is possible that some of the syntactical confusion may be due to textual complexity – scribal and revisional – it is still evident that the poet found a fairly loose syntax the most congenial mode of expressing some of his definitely complex lines of thought. The confusion possible as a result of this loose syntax is obvious to any reader of the poem. One need go no further than ll. 100-106 of the Prologue to see this:

> I parceyued of þe power . þat Peter had to kepe,
> To bynde and to vnbynde . as þe boke telleth,
> How he it left wiþ loue . as owre lorde hight,
> Amonges foure vertues . þe best of all vertues,
> Þat cardinales ben called . & closyng ȝatis,
> Þere crist is in kyngdome . to close and to shutte,
> And to opne it to hem . and heuene blisse shewe.

---

[2]   Cf. John Lawlor, *Piers Plowman: an Essay in Criticism* (London, 1962), pp. 265-274, and Bernard Huppé, "*Petrus id est Christus*: Word Play in *Piers Plowman*, the B Text", *ELH*, XVII (1950), 163-190, for further discussion of word play. – All references to *Piers Plowman* in my text are from the edition ed. W. W. Skeat (Oxford, 1886), 2 vol., and, unless otherwise noted, refer to the B-text.

The sentence structure here is, to say the least, confusing, yet it is really quite clear if the reader will just allow himself to be swept along on the train of thought: one thing suggests another. Here again is a type of logic which appears to be illogical. The similarity to dream logic is obvious, particularly in view of the fact that the whole passage hinges – if I may be permitted the expression – on the pun on "cardinales". Furthermore, this sort of loose association of ideas and words leads to a dreamlike effect in another way; as Charles Muscatine put it, "His style produces a hallucinatory effect, in which the distinctions between abstract and concrete, moral and physical, have all but been lost."[3]

Yet, in spite of what appears to be a complete removal from the real, waking world, the dreamer is always basically concerned with real life, with everyday reality. This is no vision of another world. As Donaldson points out, the dreamer "never succeeded in getting out of sight of the Field of Folk", except for the Harrowing of Hell scene; even the garden in which the Tree of Charity grows is "Cor Hominis".[4] This is part of the essential difference between *Pearl* and *Piers Plowman*: the former is a prophetic vision, making use of symbolism, the latter an allegory, transmuting familiar scenes into symbols and *vice versa*. The world of Langland's visions is the world of his everyday interests – suitably translated into the language of dreams and symbolism.

The scenes may be metaphorical, but they concern the dreamer's waking interests just as definitely as the dream of *Pearl*, and in a more literally down-to-earth fashion. In this way, the dreams are psychologically motivated in their content, just as are most literary dreams of the period. The behavior of the dreamer himself is also consistent with the facts of dream psychology and with the treatment of other medieval literary dreamers: he is constantly in a state of confusion or bemusement, constantly unable to grasp what is going on. Donaldson, comparing him to "Chaucer the Pilgrim", in an article of that title detailing his theory of the pilgrim Chaucer as "the fallible first person singular", says: "he is related to Long Will of *Piers Plowman*, a more explicit seeker after the good, but just as unswerving in his inability correctly to evaluate what he sees".[5] As noted above, the bemusement of the Pearl's Jeweler is significant in relation to the fact that he is a

---

[3] *Chaucer and the French Tradition* (Berkeley, 1957), p. 101.
[4] E. Talbot Donaldson, *Piers Plowman: The C-Text and Its Poet* (New Haven, 1949), p. 121. Cf. Lawlor, pp. 252-253.
[5] *PMLA*, LXIX (1954), p. 934.

dreamer; the same thing would appear to be true in the case of Langland's dreamer, as also with Chaucer's various dreamers.[6]

The most obvious difference between *Piers Plowman* and the other dream visions of the period is that *Piers Plowman* is not just one dream, but a series of dreams. This complicates matters, to say the least, but it also raises some rather interesting questions; in particular, there is the question of differentiation between the dreams and the passages which intervene, when the poet is talking about his waking life. This is a very vexing question for two reasons: first, some of the elements in the "waking" scenes are strictly allegorical; second, it is sometimes quite a question whether the poet has not been confused and forgotten to go to sleep, or wake up. The second question presents little difficulty in the B-text if we accept two of the visions as being dreams-within-dreams, rather than separate visions. Robert W. Frank, Jr., has made a very clear case for so understanding the visions which occur in the B-text from XI. 5-396 and XVI. 20-166.[7] In both cases the dreamer is already asleep and dreaming, but says he went to sleep without indicating any prior waking; and in both cases when he wakes up again it is into a dream-world still: in the first case, to his encounter with "Ymagynatyf", and in the second to meet Abraham. These situations are perfectly reasonable, providing that we remember in both cases that they *are* "inner dreams", and that the poet is thus still dreaming when he "wakes up" from them. That this was intended is proved by the fact that the poet subsequently "wakes up" again, and this time into the real world. This is interestingly observant dream psychology: we frequently dream that we have just been aroused from a dream, when we have simply gone into another phase of dreaming,[8] and this is certainly not a unique case of a dream-within-a-dream in medieval literature. Dante, for example, has several "inner dreams" within the vision which is the *Divine Comedy*.[9]

[6] It is noteworthy that Chaucer's dreamers precede, in the canon of his works, the "narrator" of the *Canterbury Tales*, and that while the latter is not a dreamer, in any literal sense, the conception of Chaucer the narrator evolved first in the dream visions; thus a character originally conceived as appropriate to the dreaming state may have been carried over in the poet's later works, modified, but still a very similar character, Cf. Coghill's remark quoted above, p. 71, n. 38. Also, on the relationship of the *General Prologue* to the dream vision as a whole, cf. J. V. Cunningham, "The Literary Form of the Prologue to the *Canterbury Tales*", *MP*, XLIX (1952), 172-181.

[7] "The Number of Visions in *Piers Plowman*", *MLN*, LXVI (1951), 309-312.

[8] Cf. Freud, *The Interpretation of Dreams*, in *Basic Writings*, ed. A. A. Brill (New York, 1938), pp. 513-514, 360.

[9] See, e.g., *Purgatorio*, IX. 1-42; XIX. 7-33; XXVII. 91-108.

However, although the waking and sleeping sequences are thus clearly differentiated from each other in the B-text, the other difficulty remains: some of the events of the waking scenes are just as allegorical as those within the various dreams. In the beginning of Pas. VIII the poet, clearly awake, is searching for an abstraction of his dreams, Dowel; in XV. 11, again awake, he is put to sleep by another abstraction, Resoun; and, most peculiarly of all, XX begins with the waking poet being berated as some length by "Need". The only reasonable explanation of all this would seem to be that the poet is using fairly simple metaphor here; in no case do these personifications lead into any extended allegory, and only in the last case does one even approach it. In VIII the poet expresses what he seeks as an abstraction, but seeks it among real men – friars. "Resoun", of XV, is only a passing reference – and at that a bridge between waking and sleep. "Need" is much more of a lapse from waking reality, but even he does not take on the aspect of a full-fledged vision: there is no physical description of him, and no conversation or response on the part of the poet which would imply a flesh-and-blood presence. It is nevertheless obvious that the differentiation between sleep and waking, symbol and reality, is perilously shaky here.

In the C-text the division between dream and the waking world is even more ambiguous. Most notably, in the passage at the beginning of Pas. VI, an addition of great general interest because of its auto-biographical content, the poet depicts a meeting and extended conversation with Conscience and Reason, characters who would certainly seem more at home within one of the dream sequences. In addition, divisions between sleeping and waking scenes are considerably obscured later on in the poem where the poet in revising had eliminated the transition to the second "inner dream", and in consequence he has the dreamer "wake up" from the dream of Abraham without his having fallen asleep. If we take the dream of Abraham as a waking event – as it most certainly appears, until we come to the end and find the poet waking from it – the line between dream and reality has really vanished in the C-text; but this is very easily explained, as Frank has conjectured, as an instance of the poet's simply forgetting that he had made the first change (i.e., that of amalgamating the main dream and the inner dream), and consequently neglecting to make appropriate changes at the end of the inner dream.[10] Perhaps it is not even necessary to term

---

[10] Frank's calculations arrive at the total of nine separate visions in the C-text, counting this scene as a separate vision; however, he does not appear to have

this a mistake or an omission on the part of the poet: it makes perfectly good sense as dream psychology as it stands. If we simply take the first "waking" as a dream experience, a transition from one dream to another, it is, perhaps, even closer to our usual experience in dreams than the inner dream which is carefully and consistently set apart from its surrounding dream.

Eliminating the Abraham scene, as it is in the C-text, from consideration as a possible waking sequence, since it so clearly turns out to be a dream, we have, then, two waking sequences which seem to trespass on the symbolic grounds of the dream scenes: the passage in both B and C where the poet meets Need and that in C where he encounters Conscience and Reason. There may, however, be a real justification for the inclusion of these scenes in the poet's waking, rather than dreaming, life. Metaphorical as they are, they refer very specifically to the immediate, physical, personal circumstances of the poet's life. That he encountered Need is another way of saying he was "metelees and monelees". These personal concerns only appear in a much larger context within the dreams; there the dreamer is concerned with the myriad implications for all mankind of need and poverty, not just with his own poverty. The waking sequences, then, provide a personal motivation for the visions which follow, and are therefore, while differently expressed, not essentially different from the waking prologues to Chaucer's dream visions. Just as Chaucer's waking interest in "love" (in itself an abstract concept!) led, he indicates, to the dream of the *Parliament of Fowls,* interests and circumstances of Long Will's life motivate dreams which explore the questions in his mind.

In the rest of the poem, the parts which are indisputably dreams, we can find examples galore of what may very likely be good dream psychology. We may call what happens confusion, discontinuity, and illogic, but we can also see "dream-work" at work. Condensation and transference, and the concomitant usual phenomena of dreams, could explain a great deal of the presumed confusion. For example, Donaldson remarks on the suddenness with which the dream-within-a-dream of the Tree of Charity "dissolves into a vision of the Nativity".[11] That there is a connection between the scenes is obvious: the introduction of the Incarnation suggests the Nativity. In a dream, the sudden shift

---

noticed that in the C-text the poet has also eliminated the waking and falling to sleep which separate the fifth and sixth visions; therefore, perhaps eight would be a more accurate count.

[11] *Piers Plowman,* p. 184.

of scene to another suggested by the earlier would not be the least bit surprising. The sudden appearance, and disappearance, of Piers at the banquet scene in C XVI. 138 ff. is equally true to the way things seem to happen in dreams. But the most important use of "dream-work" as a poetic device here may be in its allowance for an individual figure representing not one but several individuals or concepts, which is precisely what seems to be the case with many of the figures in Long Will's dreams. Piers himself is quite definitely at least three figures in one: the peasant Piers, Christ, and St. Peter. He may, in addition, incorporate other concepts and figures. Chambers suggests that Piers, as equalling Peter, represents the three ways of life taught by the church.[12] Coulton feels that as Peter he also represents the popes,[13] and Donaldson suggests that in the Do-Well portion of the C-text he stands "in the anagogical sense" for the prophets awaiting Christ's coming.[14] Even all these by no means exhaust the possibilities suggested by the figure of Piers;[15] but he is not only an incorporative figure. Some of his attributes are also shared by other figures – Patience, for example,[16] and Conscience; so that not only is any one figure possibly a fusion of several figures or ideas, but also one set of attributes may belong to several different figures. Thus, "splitting" and transference exist alongside condensation. For example, man, as Donaldson remarks (p. 187), is "thrice represented – once in Piers, once in the fruit of the tree, and once by Liberum Arbitrium" in the Tree of Charity scene.

An interesting example of the fusion of two dream figures is the identification of Recklessness with the dreamer in C XII. Donaldson, having noted the double meaning of Recklessness,[17] remarks: "C was careful that the reader should see through it and perceive at once the Dreamer and Recklessness. . . . I suggest that C was having a sort of double-edged joke, first in the loose identification of the Dreamer with Recklessness, second in the surprising development of Recklessness from one who is made to appear a very bad actor to one who exemplifies, to some extent, the virtue of patient poverty. I do not think

[12] R. W. Chambers, *Man's Unconquerable Mind* (Philadelphia, 1953), Chs. IV and V. He sees Christ as also living all three lives, and hence the identification with Christ.
[13] G. G. Coulton, *Medieval Panorama: the English Scene From Conquest to Reformation* (New York, 1955), Ch. 41.
[14] *Piers Plowman*, p. 180.
[15] See, e.g., Donaldson, p. 184-187.
[16] Donaldson calls Patience "Piers's *alter ego*."
[17] I.e., "recklessness of wanhope" and "reck-less-ness of St. Francis".

that Joyce was the first artist to discover that a pun might both be
entertaining and at the same time accomplish a serious purpose." [18]
This provides a fine example of dreamlike use of double meaning, both
in the language and in the lack of definite boundaries between the two
dream figures.

There are other examples of characters who are not quite separable
in the poem.[19] This works out with astonishing appropriateness in the
case of the Seven Deadly Sins: each one incorporates aspects of other
sins. Lechery and Wrath are gluttonous, Envy is wrathful, Gluttony is
slothful, Sloth is both wrathful and lecherous, and so forth. A theolo-
gian would certainly agree that this is in line with the nature of sin; [20]
a psychologist, that it is of the nature of dreams. The slipperiness of
these figures is particularly notable in the case of Envy, where what
starts out to be a male character seems to be a woman later on.[21]
Frank calls this "merely his way of showing envy at work among both
men and women",[22] which is no doubt part of the poets purpose, but
not necessarily the only one.

Robert E. Kaske remarks of the "symbols" in this poem that, as a
variety of "figurative language", they have the characteristic of "flexi-
bility or fluidity in their structure; and much intermingling both with
non-figurative material and with one another. ... the symbolism in
the poem expresses several levels of meaning through a single character
or set of events, as well as indicating connections among these various
levels." [23] But he also points out that they have the quality of con-
creteness. One aspect blending into, and reinforcing, not excluding,
another is a dominant characteristic of this poem. Speirs is making a

[18]   Page 174. – And note that *Finnegans Wake* is a dream.
[19]   For example, Donaldson points out the confusion in both C and B when, in
the latter, Warren Wisdom and Witty become Wisdom and Warren Witty, while
in the former Warren Wiseman and Wilyman (suing Wilyman, Wittyman and
Warren Wringlaw) are followed in turns by Wit and Wisdom; Wit and Wiles;
"a wise man"; Wit; and Wisdom. (C V, B IV.) Donaldson suggests that they are
meant to be interchangeable and indistinguishable, as also Favel and False;
pp. 69-70.
[20]   Cf. Chaucer's Parson's somewhat drastic remedy for lechery: "specially to
withdrawen swiche thynges as yeve occasion to thilke vileynye, as ese, etynge and
drynkynge". *Parson's Tale*, l. 951; p. 260 in Robinson.
[21]   N.b. esp. l. 110, "And biholde how Eleyne hath a newe cote", as against
the A-text's "Hou Heyne hath a newe cote and his wyf another".
[22]   Robert Worth Frank, Jr., "The Art of Reading Medieval Personification-
Allegory", *ELH*, XX (1953), p. 247.
[23]   "The Nature and Use of Figurative Expression in *Piers Plowman*, Text B",
Research in Progress, Univ. of No. Carolina Record, Grad. Sch. Series no. 60
(Oct. 1951), p. 132.

similar observation when he comments on the relation of the "wilderness" where the poet is in the Prologue, a "wilderness of the spirit",
and those in which knight wanders in romances; it is, he says, a combination of realism and symbolism. The location is real London, but
also mankind in the world. He feels it is wrong to try to make the poem
"make sense"; the poet is making "use of language that is essentially
poetic", not philosophical prose.[24]

But of course the poem makes a good deal of poetic "sense", and
its connection with the everyday sort of common sense is that it makes
sense as a dream. The dream suggests, it does not give clear answers;[25]
if *Piers Plowman* does not end by giving an answer to all the questions
raised, we must remember that it is a poem, and a dream, not a tract.
Then, too, the characteristic befuddlement of the dreamer permits him
to revert to questions that have presumably been answered again and
again, just as does the dreamer of *Pearl*.

The dream gives an excuse for all of these aspects of the poem –
and more besides; waking up, for example, serves as a way to termi-
nate a sequence with which the poet has gone as far as he wishes.[26]
Of course, the frequency with which the dreamer wakes up and goes
back to sleep not only serves to extricate the poet from his material,
so he can go on to something else without the need of tying up loose
ends, but also is a constant reminder to his audience that this is a
dream. This reminder seems absolutely necessary, in view of the complex and confusing nature of the various visions. The poet either could
not or would not take the trouble to make his work finished and tidy,[27]
and he therefore used the dream as a glorious excuse to spread out
the products of his vast imagination.

How else than as a series of dreams could he have treated such
material and yet anchored it to "real life"?

---

[24] John Speirs, *Medieval English Poetry: the Non-Chaucerian Tradition* (London, 1957), pp. 35-36, n.

[25] Cf. Jung's remark, quoted on p. 59.

[26] J. A. W. Bennett (*The Parlement of Foules* [Oxford, 1957], p. 69) compares
Langland's dropping of the Fair Field and leaving the king and knights in the
church to Africanus' disappearance in the *Parliament of Fowls*; they are not
actually comparable, however, since the disappearance of Africanus takes place
within the dream.

[27] Morton W. Bloomfield (*Piers Plowman as a Fourteenth-century Apocalypse*
[New Brunswick, N.J., 1962], p. 6) suggests one reason why the poet could not
have made his work "perfect" in an artistic sense: "his aim is to show the spiritual
confusion of his own times. Spiritual confusion demands to some extent artistic
confusion".

VIII

TWO LESSER DREAM VISIONS

The two remaining fourteenth century dream visions are the *Parliament of the Three Ages* [1] and *Winner and Waster*. [2] In the case of the *Parliament,* there does not appear to be anything at all in the content or treatment of the dream which could not have been presented as an observation of a waking encounter, except for the designation of the three dream figures as abstractions – i.e., they are *named* "Youth", "Middle Age", and "Age". They could just as easily be named Tom, Dick, and Harry, who happen to be of three different generations. The most interesting aspect of these figures is the picture of the life of the period we get from the statements of Youth and Middle Age. The ultimate purpose of the scene seems to be simply to provide an excuse for telling stories about the Nine Worthies. The dream, therefore, does not appear to be allegory in any significant sense; perhaps it would be more interesting if it were.

This may, however, be an unfair estimate of the poem. If we could be more sure of the meaning of the prologue – that is, of its connection, or lack of it, with the dream that follows – perhaps the dream would appear in a totally different light. It is possible that the poet may have been implying a great deal in the hunting scene which eludes us because we do not have the same associations with deer, or with hunting. There are a number of possibilities along this line; for example, the bestiaries' frequent association of deer with longevity and regeneration may have something to do with the problem of age. According to one twelfth century bestiary, 'to estimate their longevity, Alexander the Great once ringed a large number of stags which, when recaptured after a hundred years, did not show signs of senility." [3] The same source reports that

---

[1] The E.E.T.S. has recently published a new edition of this poem, *The Parlement of the Thre Ages*, ed. M. Y. Offord (Oxford, 1959).

[2] *Wynnere and Wastoure*, ed. I Gollanz (London, 1920), is the standard edition.

[3] T. H. White, *The Book of Beasts: Being a Translation from a Latin Bestiary of the Twelfth Century* (New York, 1954), p. 39.

stags, "after a dinner of snake, ... shed their coats and all their old age with them".[4] The account goes on to tell us that eating venison can make people "immortal and immune to fevers", but cautions that this is not infallible – a wound can still be fatal. A Middle English bestiary tells us that the stag renews life by shedding his horns:

> oc he werped er hise hornes
> in wude er in ðornes,
> *and* gingið him ðus ðis wilde der
> so ge hauen nu lered her.[5]

The moral is that we should cast off pride and thus renew our lives.[6]

Or, the significance of the hunting scene could hinge on some observation current among hunters in the period about the habits of the animal. Henry L. Savage has written on the authenticity of the various hunting and nature references.[7] The fact that the hart has a companion, for example, may be based on observation of the habits of deer,[8] and may have given rise to explanations which did not find their way into the bestiaries. Again, there are hundreds of medieval stories of a more mystical nature concerning deer. The eighteenth tale of the *Gesta Romanorum* is the story of a knight to whom a stag he was pursuing turned and predicted that he would kill his parents – which he did. Many saints' legends involve deer. St. Idda used a stag as a candle! (He had flames shooting up from his horns, it seems.) Various saints succoured stags fleeing hunters, or were converted by the holy behavior of stags. The best known of these legends is that of St. Eustace, to whom a stag appeared with a cross between his antlers.[9]

Speirs makes an interesting statement on this question: "Most likely the slaying of the deer was the way to secure a vision or dream-guidance. Alfred Nutt, the folklorist, noted instances from Grail and Mabinogi legends of the hero hunting a stag, slaying it and falling under

---

[4] *Ibid.*, p. 38.

[5] *An Old English Miscellany, Containing a Bestiary, Kentish Sermons, Proverbs of Alfred, Religious Poems of the Thirteenth Century*, ed. Richard Morris (London, 1872), p. 11.

[6] The account includes the "fact" that the stag eats snakes, but does not connect this with rejuvenation.

[7] "Notes on the Prologue of the Parliament of the Thre Ages", *JEGP*, XXIX (1930), pp. 74-82.

[8] Cf. Edward of Norwich, *The Master of Game*, ed. William A. and F. Baillie-Grohman (London, 1909), p. 26.

[9] See S. Baring-Gould, *The Lives of the Saints* (Edinburgh, 1914), 16 vol.; the story of St. Eustace appears in the September volume, p. 319. – Cf. the story about St. Julian related in *Sir Gawain and the Green Knight*, ed. J. R. R. Tolkien and E, V. Gordon (Oxford, 1955), l. 774, and n., p. 95.

an 'illusion' in consequence; the stag was a regular messenger from the faery world and thus passed into Christian hagiology." [10] While Speirs is apt to exaggerate the mythological element in medieval literature, this is a temptingly interesting conjecture on the meaning of this passage. It is, however, far from conclusive; so that in the end we must still admit we cannot be sure what the prologue implies, and therefore cannot fix its relationship to the dream. This is, of course, a pity; for if we knew what the dream connection was it might shed a good deal of light on the meaning of the poem, or, at least, on the poet's ability to organize and relate his materials.

Even more baffling is the significance of the prologue to *Winner and Waster*. The poem as a whole, if it can be called a whole, is infinitely baffling, but perhaps more interesting than the *Parliament of the Three Ages* on that account. It is strongly reminiscent of various other poems; so much so that (although it is possibly vice-versa) it seems almost certain the poet must have known *Piers Plowman*, and may have known others of the poems here discussed. The first lines bring *Gawain and the Green Knight* immediately to mind; then, the mention of "witt and wylle" and "wyli wordes" reminds us of *Piers Plowman*, a reminiscence which is reinforced by the prophecy which follows, and by the close resemblance in wording of the actual dream opening. However, unlike the dreams of *Piers Plowman*, there is no clear indication of the connection between the complaints voiced in the poet's waking person and his dream.

This is by no means the only problem which confronts us in this poem. For one thing, it is unfinished; for another, it appears to be a "Garter poem", but it is not at all clear what these references mean, or how they connect with the battle – or debate – which follows. With these and other difficulties befogging the issues, it may seem hardly worth while to attempt any careful analysis of this poem. Nevertheless, it is worth noting that some of its confusion is the same sort of thing we have seen in other dream visions, particularly the difficulty in sorting out the characters, one from another, and the fact that they seem to be constantly taking on new and apparently strange associations. It is particularly interesting that while the opposing forces, as originally described, would seem to array the various ranks of the Church along with the merchant class on Winner's side, as against

[10] *Medieval English Poetry: the Non-Chaucerian Tradition* (London, 1957), p. 292.

what appears to be the nobility, this division breaks down in the course of the debate, when Waster defends the rights of "prelates" and "prowde marchandes of pris" to live in high style,[11] thus appropriating to his own side part of what was presumably the enemy camp. Perhaps this rather dreamlike shift symbolizes the usual medieval dichotomy between the ideal of the church and its actuality, and includes the merchant class as being also, in its way, turncoat.

But also, the ending of the poem takes a very startling turn: the king's advice to Winner is that he go and enjoy pleasures that would seem more in Waster's line:

> Wende, wynnere, þe waye ouer þe wale stremys,
> Passe forthe by Paris to þe Pope of Rome;
> The cardynalls ken þe wele, will kepe þe ful faire,
> & make þi sydes in silken schetys to lygge,
> & fede þe & foster þe & forthir thyn hert,
> As leefe to worthen wode as þe to wrethe ones.[12]

Waster, on the other hand, is told to go to Cheapside, and given directions on how to get people to buy various things. The two would seem to be changing roles almost completely; so that it is very hard to understand what can be meant when the king goes on to say, "þe more þu wastis þi wele, þe better þe wynner lykes" (l. 495).

In view of all this, Baugh's statement that the king's advice is for each to go his own way is rather questionable.[13] Who is going which way? But another statement of Baugh's is indubitably true: "The meaning of the two hosts and their constituents is not very clear." [14]

In any case, we cannot complain that this poem is not dreamlike. Only a dream could be so fluid in its personnel. Clearly, the poet is taking advantage of the form he has chosen. But the reader is led to suspect that this advantage is mainly, for this poet, that the dream allows him an excuse for incoherence. If he had been writing anything other than a dream, he might have had to take a good many more pains to make himself clear.

Several points stand out when we compare these two poems with the other fourteenth century Middle English dream visions. First, it is obvious that they make use of most of the familiar conventions of the form – the May opening, flowers, birds, etc. are present, as are the

---

[11] Lines 376-377.
[12] Lines 460-465.
[13] "The Middle English Period", in *A Literary History of England*, ed. A. C. Baugh (New York, 1948), p. 241.
[14] Page 240, n.

narrator's opening remarks introducing his dream. It is, futhermore, possible that the poet (/poets) knew and drew on other contemporary poems of the genre, as witness the similarity of wording to that of *Piers Plowman*, e.g. in ll. 1-2 of the *Parliament*.[15] But, on the other hand, they are unique in omitting one otherwise universal feature of the fourteenth century Middle English dream vision: in neither of these poems does the dreamer take any active part in the action or dialogue. The narrator simply relates what he saw and heard. While there are passages in all the other dream visions discussed above which are simply reports of what the dreamer saw or overheard, eventually the dreamer takes some part in the scene – *Pearl*'s Jeweler tries to fling himself into the river, Chaucer's presence is discovered and he must come forth and speak.

This omission of the figure of the dreamer actively participating in his dream may have significant bearing on the less satisfactory qualities of the two poems. For example, the actions and reactions of the dreamers in the other poems serve as unifying devices, relating the dream to the preliminary material in a way which is sorely lacking in both these cases.

It is, then, clear that while the dream form was in some way a help to the poet (or poets), in this respect, as well as in others, he (or they) fell short, in comparison to the other poets who used the form. Each of the great poets found a way to use the dream really effectively. This cannot be said to be the case with those two confusing poems, *Winner and Waster* and the *Parliament of the Three Ages*.

---

[15] Perhaps, too, the hunting scene which opens that poem may owe something to the hunt in the *Book of the Duchess*. But, of course, whether such influences are possible depends on the date of the poem, which is still not by any means a matter of general agreement. It may be that, as Gollanz thought (see his preface to *Winner and Waster*, last paragraph), the author of *Piers Plowman* was the borrower rather than vice versa.

IX

THE DREAM AS A VEHICLE FOR ALLEGORY

In almost every case the Middle English dream poems of the fourteenth century made use of blending, fusion, double-meaning: of the
characteristics we have seen to be typical of this genre, and know to
be typical of dreams. These are also highly characteristic of most
medieval allegory and symbolism, and this may have a good deal to
do with the popularity of the dream form in this period. The purposes
of the dream form in Middle English poetry seem to have been mul-
tiple, and to include the various purposes previously suggested. Authority, for one thing, was certainly one of the desiderata of the poet
choosing this form, especially if his material was supernatural, and
also if it was controversial. Since it was an accepted "fact" that dreams
were sometimes divine revelations, and, therefore, true visions of the
future or the hereafter, a poet such as the author of *Pearl* could claim
that his audience did not have to take his unsupported word for all that
theology – God had dictated the content of his dream. The dream
vision had a double authority: the assertion of the poet that he really
saw all this in a dream, and the support of the writers and theologians,
both classical and Christian, who had proclaimed the possibility of such
a revelation. And at the same time, this took the pressure off the poet.
He could not be held personally responsible for the contents of a dream,
something quite beyond his conscious control, whether or not the
manuscript was divinely dictated.[1]

[1] Morton W. Bloomfield (*Piers Plowman as a Fourteenth-century Apocalypse*
[New Brunswick, N. J., 1962], p. 12) maintains that medieval literary dreams are
to be understood exclusively as vehicles of divine thought; thus, he argues, "We
cannot blame or defend Langland's lack of order because of his use of the dream
form ... or explain the disappearance of the dog in Chaucer's *Book of the
Duchess* on the same grounds." The present study attempts to show that such
an either/or view is not necessary: that medieval dream visions may be presented
as divinely inspired, or psychologically motivated, or both – or theoretically
neither, one supposes. The grounds for regarding indications of dream psychology
as deliberate in Chaucer (e.g., that dog) seem particularly cogent.

Of course it was equally well-known that dreams could have psychological origins, and were not uniformly reliable. The poet who made use of this information had, as we have seen, an excellent motivating device, as well as an alternate explanation for scoffers; the poet could claim, as the *Pearl*-poet does, that both aspects are true in the case of this particular dream. Alternatively, he could plead ignorance, as Chaucer did in the *House of Fame* and the *Parliament of Fowls*, and leave it up to the reader to decide how seriously the dream is to be taken. The realistic, psychological aspects of the dream were, as we have also seen, useful to the poet in many ways, and various poets made various uses of these aspects.

The most usual effect of dream-work in these poems is the possibility of multifold and shifting meaning, and multifold and shifting meanings are exactly the characteristics of medieval allegory and symbolism in general. The complex possibilities of layers of meaning in a dream offer a fine opportunity for the layers of meaning medieval commentators searched for in scripture and in poetry. Allegory does not necessarily mean simply "an extended simile", as the word is defined in one current dictionary.[2] E. K. Rand summarizes the meaning of allegory, as passed down from St. Ambrose to Dante, as, "the four varieties of meanings that might attend a verse of scripture or a poet's verse – the *sensus morales,* their application to human character; *sensus allegoricus* or *mysticus,* the prophecy of the Gospels in some passage of the Old Testament; and the *sensus anagogicus,* which revealed something about man's experience in the life to come."[3]

This idea of the "fourfold method" was to be applied, properly speaking, only to Scripture, according to St. Thomas, as Professor Charles Donahue pointed out in a paper delivered to the English Institute in September, 1958.[4] The difference is, of course, that, as St. Thomas said, "the author of Holy Writ is God, in Whose power it is

[2] *Funk and Wagnell's College Standard Dictionary* (New York, 1946), p. 36.
[3] *Founders of the Middle Ages* (New York, 1928), p. 86.
[4] "Patristic Exegesis in the Criticism of Medieval Literature: Summation", *Critical Approaches to Medieval Literature: Selected Papers from the English Institute, 1958-59,* ed. Dorothy Bethurum (New York, 1960), pp. 61-82; cf. *Questiones quod liberales,* vii. Prof. Donahue discussed this question further in a paper delivered to the Medieval Club of New York in December 1958, remarking that Dante's statements in the *Convivio* and the letter to Can Grande, which are of great importance since he was the only medieval poet to claim fourfold allegory in his own work, are not actually consistent, and probably represent the poet's attempt, in looking back, to examine and explain what he had done, rather than a plan he had definitely held in his mind at the time of actual composition.

to signify His meaning, not by words only (as man also can do), but also by things themselves. So, whereas in every other science things are signified by words, this science has the property that the things signified by the words have themselves also a signification. Therefore that first signification whereby words signify things belongs to the first interpretation, the historical or literal. That signification whereby things signified by words have themselves also a signification is called the spiritual interpretation, which is based on the literal interpretation and presupposes it. Now this spiritual interpretation has a threefold division." [5] Poetry, in St. Thomas's view, does not have at all the same purpose: "Poetry makes use of metaphors to produce a picture, for it it natural to man to be pleased with pictures. But Sacred Science makes use of metaphors as both useful and necessary." [6]

Nevertheless, poetry does make use of metaphor, and whenever it does it is making use of allegory, according to the classical definition of Cassiodorus: "Allegoria est enim, sicut saepe jam dictum est, quando aliud dicitur, et aliud significatur." [7] To say one thing but mean something else is a simple definition which is always true – as far as it goes – of medieval allegory. Even Biblical exegesis was often on this comparatively simple level; Paul Pickrel has remarked that the fourfold method was by no means universal even in this area. Many preachers before 1250 discussed only one allegorical level, and interest in the fourfold method waned perceptibly in the later period.[8] But the fact remains that the fourfold method was widely popular in the thirteenth and fourteenth centuries; and it does not seem unreasonable to suspect that the spirit of it would be apt to be carried over into secular poetry. Men who were used to being told from the pulpit that various texts had one or more meanings besides the literal would naturally tend to think of their own poetry in similar terms.

It is to be noted that all, or some, of these "senses" were expected to exist simultaneously; one did not rule out another. As Erich Auerbach remarked, "In this connection an occurrence on earth signifies not only itself but at the same time another, which it predicts or con-

[5] *Summa Theologica*, trans. Fathers of the English Dominican Province (London, 1916), vol. I, p. 17; I, i, 10.

[6] *Ibid.*, p. 15; i, 9.

[7] Migne, *Pat. Lat.*, 70, col. 223. Cf. the derivation of the word "allegory" cited by Paul M. Pickrel, *Religious Allegory in Medieval England: an Introductory Study Based on the Vernacular Sermon Before 1250* (unpublished Yale diss., 1944), p. 11. Other patristic definitions of allegory can be found in Migne, *Pat. Lat.*, 219, Index XLVI, cols. 123 ff.

[8] *Op. cit.*, pp. 50-51, 84.

firms, *without prejudice to the power of its concrete reality here and now"* (italics added).[9] Then, as allegory could mean two or more things simultaneously, not just one thing symbolized by another, perhaps the dream was the logical ultimate vehicle for it.

It seems quite possible that such dreams as *Pearl* and *Piers Plowman* have meanings corresponding to a *sensus moralis* and a *sensus anagogicus*, as well as a *sensus literalis*; but it may be very difficult to disentangle them at any given moment. That four definite, separate levels cannot be located and isolated in these poems seems to have been demonstrated by those who have attempted to do just that. The futility of the attempt is obvious when the most enthusiastic proponents of fourfold interpretation cannot agree on what the four senses are in their analyses of the same poem, as is the case with *Pearl*. D. W. Robertson states: "Literally, the Pearl is a gem. Allegorically, as the maiden of the poem, it represents those members of the Church who will be among the 'hundred' in the celestial procession, the perfectly innocent. Tropologically, the Pearl is a symbol of the soul that attains innocence through true penance and all that such penance implies. Anagogically, it is the life of innocence in the Celestial City." [10] William J. Knightley differs significantly: while he feels that the maiden represents the Church, he sees the tropological meaning as Adam and the fall of man, and the anagogical as the mysteries of the Church.[11]

The allegory and symbolism of *Piers Plowman* and *Pearl* are slippery and shifting, as is a dream, and, it seems to me, they have a very real validity as an artistic representation of dream experience, although in a rather different sense from the sort of dream experience Chaucer capitalizes upon in the *Book of the Duchess*. Still, these uses are related. *Pearl* uses some of the same sort of dream experiences Chaucer portrayed: the ease with which the "jeweler" climbs the hills of the dream landscape, for example, is comparable to the fluid transition from chamber to forest in the *Book of the Duchess*. But also Chaucer, while not writing "allegory" in the sense in which *Piers Plowman* is

---

[9] *Mimesis* (New York, 1957), p. 490; cf. G. G. Coulton, *Medieval Faith and Symbolism* (New York, 1958), p. 294.
[10] "The Pearl as a Symbol", *MLN*, LXV (1950), p. 160.
[11] "Symbolic Imagery in Pearl", *DA*, XVII (June, 1957), 1339-40. Coghill has similarly argued for a fourfold interpretation of *Piers Plowman* in his introduction to Wells' translation, p. xvii; this has been sharply challenged by Robert W. Frank, Jr., "The Art of Reading Medieval Personification Allegory", *ELH*, XX (1953), 249-250, and John Lawlor, *Piers Plowman; an Essay in Criticism* (London, 1962), pp. 265-274, and pp. 240-245.

allegory, uses symbols and dream figures much as Langland and the *Pearl*-poet did, notably in the case of the lady of the Prologue to the *Legend of Good Women*. Chaucer may not have been writing formal allegory, but he was using some of the techniques of allegory; perhaps at least partially because they also are the techniques of dream, and he was writing dream visions.

Gordon states that "a modern poet would indeed be very unlikely to put forward for factual acceptance a dream that in any way resembled the vision of *Pearl*"; [12] but the reason for this is that we think in terms of a different *kind* of symbolism today. It is still an accepted fact, and one of the fundamentals of modern psychiatry, that dreams use symbols, and that, by means of this symbolism, they may reveal truths which are obscured to the waking mind.

But just as the truths revealed in dream are often far from clear, symbolism in the Middle Ages was not simple and systematic. As Coulton remarks, "the equivocal nature of symbolic teaching is proverbial; one of the best and most natural of ancient stories is that of James VI and the Professor of Signs". [13] We have seen some of the enormous variety of meanings assigned to the pearl by various writers; the same thing is true of the significances attached to all sorts of gems and animals, as any bestiary or lapidary makes clear. [14] In view of this diversity, how are we to tell what the author of a particular work meant us to understand in his use of various symbols and images? Practically any element of a medieval allegory may have more than one possible meaning, though critics who argue for one implication have frequently scorned all alternative suggestions. [15]

One principle to apply here is plain common sense: some of the possible associations of a given symbol may be quite out of place in a particular context. For example, we can hardly entertain the notion that the *Pearl*-poet intended any association of his Pearl with earthly delights and the Whore of Babylon. [16] Nor does it seem to this writer at all likely that the lover's plucking of the rose in the *Romance of the*

---

[12] Introduction to *Pearl* (Oxford, 1953), p. xv.

[13] *Op. cit.*, p. 319; Coulton gives the story of the Professor of Signs in Appendix 24, pp. lxv-lxvi. This concerns two men conversing through signs, both absolutely sure of the meaning of the signs, but actually having a totally different interpretation.

[14] Cf. Coulton, pp. 270 ff. and lii.

[15] See, e.g., Ian Bishop, "The Significance of the 'Garlande Gay' in the Allegory of *Pearl*", *RES*, VIII, 12-21; cf. Gordon, p. xxxi.

[16] Cf. above, n. 11, p. 65.

Rose is intended to imply the Fall of Man, as one recent dissertation maintains.[17] But even after eliminating the impossible and the implausible we are still often left with a welter of possible implications. Speirs has commented on the rich and multifarious meanings of favorite medieval symbols; for example, the tree may mean Christ, the Tree of Life, the Tree of Jesse; or the Tree of Evil; its boughs may signify virtues, or the elect, or the Seven Beatitudes. He goes on to remark: "The same image may mean different things in different contexts, and it may mean several things at one and the same time in the same context." [18] He applies this to medieval symbolism in general, painting and sculpture as well as poetry. Medieval symbolism does not seem to be intelligible in terms of one-to-one correspondences. Along this same line, Donaldson remarks: "The objection that within Chaucer's dream [Prologue to the *Legend of Good Women*] Alceste could not symbolize Anne because Alceste's injunction mentions Anne as a distinct person is based on a mistaken notion of the consistency required by medieval allegory: within the fiction Anne and Alceste may be one and the same, but this does not preclude Anne's having, outside of the poem, a real existence which the poem recognizes." [19] Strict logic is just not to be expected in medieval allegory. It is no wonder that the allegorists found the dream such a congenial medium.[20]

Many commentators have expressed an almost contrary view of allegory. Miss Hammond comments: "Rigid itself, allegory links readily with those devices for expression which are rigid." [21] But the dream vision form, one of the "devices" commonly used for allegory, was, as used by the poets discussed above, anything but rigid. But then, Miss Hammond was not concentrating on those poets: this remark was

---

[17]   Charles R. Dahlberg, "The Secular Tradition in Chaucer and Jean de Meun", *DA*, XIV (1954), p. 121; cf. D. W. Robertson, Jr., "The Doctrine of Charity in Medieval Literary Gardens: a Topical Approach Through Symbolism and Allegory," *Speculum*, XXVI (1951), 24-49.
[18]   John Speirs, *Medieval English Poetry: the Non-Chaucerian Tradition* (London, 1957), pp. 389-390.
[19]   *Chaucer's Poetry* (New York, 1958), p. 958; cf. Frank, p. 249.
[20]   Another aspect of the usefulness of the dream is suggested by H. B. Willson, "Walther's Dream", *MLR*, LIII (April, 1958), 191-196. Commenting on mystic and trinitarian aspects of a poem in which the poet wakes from a dream of happiness to the cawing of a crow, he observes that Middle High German poetry was fond of the unity-in-plurality theme, which while not always religious in context derives from the "reconciliation of antitheses" of Christian thought. The dream is, of course, a fitting place for the reconciliation of antitheses.
[21]   Eleanor Prescott Hammond, *English Verse Between Chaucer and Surrey* (Durham, 1927), p. 29.

made in an anthology of poetry between Chaucer and Surrey – the
poetry of the fifteenth century, which is quite a different matter. Allegory and dream are all too common features of fifteenth century English poetry, but they are not used in the same ways. A look at a few
of the many fifteenth century descendents of the dream vision shows
any number of differences.

The best of these poems turn the conventions and patterns of the
medieval dream vision to quite new uses. Henryson begins the *Testament of Cresseid* with something very like the usual "May morning"
opening, but, as Marshall Stearns has pointed out, with a difference:
it is not a dream at all, and the season is definitely wintry (although it
is April), with bad weather, suitable to the mood of the poet.[22] But,
while the poem is not a dream vision, the most important action in it,
the condemnation of Cresseid, takes place within a dream.[23] Similarly,
the *Kingis Quair* is not a dream, but it contains a very long, allegorical
dream, comprising a vision of great importance to the dreamer.[24] These
poems, among the best of their century, represent new developments
of the dream idea. The influence of the dream vision is obvious, but
the dreams are metaphorical in a rather different sense, containing as
they do premonitions of an important crisis in the lives of the dreamers.
Perhaps they are more closely akin to Criseyde's dream in the *Troilus*
than to the dream visions of the fourteenth century. This particular
affinity is scarcely surprising, however, considering the fact that
Chaucer is, for both poets, the dominant influence (and, in the first
case at least, Chaucer's *Troilus*), and Chaucer himself not only abandoned the use of the dream as framework in his later works, using
dreams only for dramatic purposes within a non-dream context, but
also appears to have regarded the dream, as a form, only as a con-
venience in organizing and unifying his poems. His lack of reverence
for the dream as a channel for divine guidance is witnessed by the fact
that in his last dream vision the divine guidance comes from the
patently incompetent "God of Love".

Other poets of this century followed the conventions of the traditional dream vision, the conventions inherited from the *Romance of*

[22]   *Robert Henryson* (New York, 1949), pp. 60-62.
[23]   Stanzas 21-49; in *Poems and Fables*, ed. H. Harvey Wood (London, 1933),
pp. 110-117.
[24]   Ed. W. Mackay Mackenzie (London, 1939), stanzas 74-172, pp. 66-94. Cf.
also John Rolland's *Court of Venus*, ii, 384-470, 778 ff., where the dreamer is
comforted by a dream; cf. C. S. Lewis, *The Allegory of Love* (London, 1938),
p. 295.

the Rose and its ilk, much more closely, but usually appear to succeed only in making us feel that they are nothing more than conventions. In the *Temple of Glass* Lydgate has some slight indication of dream psychology,[25] as does Dunbar in the *Golden Targe*;[26] but these seem strictly derivative, so close to obvious models that the poets hardly deserve credit for any fresh observation. Lydgate, in another poem, holds on to all the other *Romance of the Rose* conventions, but discards the dream itself.[27] Dunbar uses dream as a framework for several other poems, but in a number of quite different ways, and mostly for satirical purposes.[28]

In the work of these poets the dream and allegory no longer have the same connections they had in earlier visions, and the most common earmarks of the dream vision genre may or may not be associated with a dream. In some cases, what purports to be a dream vision is neither dreamlike nor allegorical. For example, Miss Ruth M. Fisher has commented that the *Assembly of Ladies* "uses personified abstractions to present a fairly realistic picture of courtly fashion and ceremonial".[29]

The reasons for these changes may be that allegory did not mean quite the same thing to the fifteenth century that it did to the fourteenth. Much of the allegory in the poems mentioned above, as well as in other fifteenth century poems, did tend to become rigid; the best known example of fifteenth century allegory, for example, is *Everyman*, a systematic allegory with an absolute one-to-one correspondence for every figure. This is not the kind of allegory used in the great fourteenth century dream visions, and this sort of allegory certainly has little or no relationship to dream psychology. Insofar as this represents a trend during this century, the connection between dream and allegory would naturally tend to seem a dead weight of convention, a form which had outlived its real purpose. The vitality of the dream form was bound to decline as allegory tended to be either more absolute and rigid or discarded in favor of "realism." The more interesting allegory of the next century, in the work of such poets as Skelton and Spenser, seems to owe at least as much to the allusive, kaleidoscopic visions of the

[25]   Ed. J. Schick (London, 1891); n.b., the sudden, dreamlike transition in l. 531.
[26]   William Dunbar, *Poems*, ed. John Small (Edinburgh, 1893), vol. 1, I.
[27]   "The Complaint of the Black Knight", in *Minor Poems*, ed. Henry Noble MacCracken (London, 1934), pp. 382-410.
[28]   See, e.g., poems nos. XXVI, XXVII, XXVIII, XXX, and XXXIII.
[29]   "The *Flower and the Leaf* and the *Assembly of Ladies*: a Study of Two Love-Vision Poems of the Fifteenth Century", *DA*, XV (1955), 1233; cf. Lewis, p. 250.

fourteenth century as to the systematic allegories which appear to be more typical of the fifteenth century.

It is, of course, dangerous to make a sharp distinction between later "realism" and the sort of allegory found in the medieval dream vision. While it may have dealt frequently with abstractions and ideals, these, whether we are talking about Langland's "Liberum Arbitrium" or Chaucer's "Nature", represent aspects of "reality" quite as significant to the poets as the routine matters of their daily life. Often they are related to daily life, but in a metaphorical way. These poems are using symbolism, and symbolism is related to dream-work.

Tindall: remarks "Taking elements commended to his notice by some similarity of function or feeling, the dreamworker combines them in one image or act. This rich composite of meanings, though designed to conceal them, invites attention by its brilliance. If symbol implies putting together, Freud's account of this unconscious work may shed light on the origins, process, and nature of literary symbolism, without, however, explaining it away; for origins do not determine things entirely, nor is likeness identity." [30] He goes on to cite examples of post-Freudian writers who have deliberately made use of dream-work as an artistic device, a method of symbolism. It is also obvious that many pre-Freudians seem to have realized a close relationship between dream-work and what they were trying to do as poets. Long after the time of the author of *Pearl*, poets have continued to be fascinated with the relationships between waking reality and the dream, and many have asked with Poe,

> Is *all* that we see or seem
> But a dream within a dream? [31]

[30]   William York Tindall, *The Literary Symbol* (Bloomington, Ind., 1955), p. 168.
[31]   "A Dream Within a Dream", in *Selected Poetry and Prose,* ed. Thomas O. Mabbott (New York, 1953), p. 10.

SELECTED BIBLIOGRAPHY

I. EDITIONS

Chaucer, Geoffrey, *The Complete Works of Geoffrey Chaucer*, ed. Walter W. Skeat, 2nd ed., 7 vol. (Oxford, 1899).
—, *The Works of Geoffrey Chaucer*, ed. F. N. Robinson, 2nd ed. (Cambridge, Mass., 1957).
—, *The Book of Troilus and Criseyde by Geoffrey Chaucer*, ed. Robert Kilburn Root (Princeton, 1926).
—, *Chaucer's Major Poetry*, ed. Albert C. Baugh (New York, 1963).
—, *Chaucer's Poetry*, ed. E. T. Donaldson (New York, 1958).
—, *The Text of the Canterbury Tales, Studied on the Basis of All Known Manuscripts*, ed. John M. Manly and Edith Rickert (Chicago, 1940).
Dunbar, William, *Poems*, ed. John Small, 3 vol. (Edinburgh, 1893).
Gower, John, *Confessio Amantis*, in *English Works*, ed. G. C. Macaulay, 2 vol. (London, 1901).
Hammond, Eleanor Prescott, ed., *English Verse Between Chaucer and Surrey* (Durham, 1927).
Henryson, Robert, *Poems and Fables*, ed. H. Harvey Wood (London, 1933).
James I, King of Scotland, *The Kingis Quair*, ed. W. Mackay Mackenzie (London, 1939).
Langland, William, *Piers Plowman: The A Version, Will's Visions of Piers Plowman and Do-Well*, ed. George Kane (Oxford, 1960).
—, *Piers the Plowman: A Critical Edition of the A-Version*, ed. Thomas A. Knott and David C. Fowler (Baltimore, 1952).
—, *The Vision of William Concerning Piers the Plowman*, ed. W. W. Skeat, 2 vol. (Oxford, 1886).
Lydgate, John, "The Complaint of the Black Knight", in *Minor Poems*, ed. Henry Noble MacCracken (London, 1934).
—, *Temple of Glas*, ed. J. Schick (London, 1891).
Machaut, Guillelme de. *Oeuvres*, ed. Ernest Hoepffner, 3 vol. (Paris, 1908).
Parlement of the Thre Ages, ed. I. Gollancz (London, 1915).
Parlement of the Thre Ages, ed. M. Y. Offord (Oxford, 1959).
Patience, A West Midland Poem of the Fourteenth Century, ed. Hartley Bateson (Manchester, 1918).
Pearl, ed. E. V. Gordon (Oxford, 1953).
Purity, a Middle English Poem, ed. Robert J. Menner (New Haven, 1920).
Rolland, John, *Ane Treatise Callit the Court of Venus*, ed. W. Gregor (Edinburgh, 1884).
Le Roman de la Rose, ed. Ernest Langlois, 5 vols. (Paris, 1912).

Le Roman de la Rose, trans. André Mary (Paris, 1949).
The Romance of the Rose, trans. F. S. Ellis, 3 vol. (London, 1900).
The Romance of the Rose, trans. Harry W. Robbins, ed. Charles W. Dunn (New York, 1962).
Sir Gawain and the Green Knight, ed. J. R. R. Tolkien and E. V. Gordon (Oxford, 1955).
Wynnere and Wastoure, ed. I. Gollanz (London, 1920).

II. DREAM PSYCHOLOGY AND PHILOSOPHY

Curry, Walter Clyde, *Chaucer and the Medieval Sciences* (New York, 1926).
Freud, Sigmund, *Basic Writings*, trans. A. A. Brill (New York, 1938).
Fromm, Erich, *The Forgotten Language: An Introduction to the Understanding of Dreams, Fairy Tales and Myths* (New York, 1951).
Jung, C[arl] G., *Modern Man in Search of a Soul*, trans. W. S. Dell and Cary F. Baynes (New York, 1933).
—, *Two Essays on Analytical Psychology*, trans. R. F. C. Hull (New York, 1956).
Macrobius, *Commentary on the Dream of Scipio*, trans. William Harris Stahl (New York, 1952).
Pike, Joseph B., ed. and trans., *Frivolities of Courtiers and Footprints of Philosophers: Being a Translation of the First, Second, and Third Books and Selections From the Seventh and Eighth Books of the Policraticus of John of Salisbury* (Minneapolis, 1938).
Thorndike, Lynn, *A History of Magic and Experimental Science During the First Thirteen Centuries of Our Era*, 2 vol. Vols. 3 and 4: *Fourteenth* and *Fifteenth Centuries* (New York, 1929-1934).
Wolff, Werner, *The Dream – Mirror of Conscience* (New York, 1952).

III. CRITICISM AND LITERARY SCHOLARSHIP

Bennett, J. A. W., *The Parlement of Foules: An Interpretation* (Oxford, 1957).
Bloomfield, Morton W., *Piers Plowman as a Fourteenth-century Apocalypse* (New Brunswick, N. J., 1962).
Bronson, Bertrand H., *In Search of Chaucer* (Toronto, 1960).
Chambers, R. W., *Man's Unconquerable Mind* (Philadelphia, 1953).
Coghill, Nevill, *The Poet Chaucer* (London, 1949).
Donaldson, E. Talbot, *Piers Plowman: the C-text and its Poet* (New Haven, 1949).
Everett, Dorothy, *Essays on Middle English Literature*, ed. Patricia Kean (Oxford, 1955).
Gunn, Alan M. F., *The Mirror of Love: a Reinterpretation of 'The Romance of the Rose'* (Lubbock, Texas, 1952).
Kittredge, G[eorge] L[yman], *Chaucer and His Poetry: Lectures Delivered in 1914 on the Percy Turnbull Memorial Foundation in the Johns Hopkins University* (Cambridge, Mass., 1924).
Langlois, Ernest, *Origines et Sources du Roman de la Rose* (Paris, 1890).
Lawlor, John, *Piers Plowman: an Essay in Criticism* (London, 1962).
Lewis, C. S., *The Allegory of Love* (London, 1948).

Lowes, John Livingston, *Geoffrey Chaucer* (Oxford, 1934).

Malone, Kemp, *Chapters on Chaucer* (Baltimore, 1951).

Muscatine, Charles, *Chaucer and the French Tradition* (Berkeley, 1957).

Neilson, William Allen, *The Origins and Sources of the 'Court of Love'* (Boston, 1899).

Oakden, J. P., *Alliterative Poetry in Middle English* (Manchester, 1935).

Patch, Howard R., *On Rereading Chaucer* (Cambridge, Mass., 1948).

Preston, Raymond, *Chaucer* (London, 1952).

Root, Robert Kilburn, *The Poetry of Chaucer: a Guide to Study and Appreciation* (New York, 1950).

Shelly, Percy Van Dyke, *The Living Chaucer* (Philadelphia, 1940).

Speirs, John, *Medieval Poetry: The Non-Chaucerian Tradition* (London, 1957).

Sypherd, W[ilbur] Owen, *Studies in Chaucer's 'Hous of Fame'* (London, 1907).

Tatlock, J. S. P., *The Mind and Art of Chaucer* (Syracuse, N. Y., 1950).

Wagenknecht, Edward, ed., *Chaucer: Modern Essays in Criticism* (New York, 1959).

INDEX

DE PROPRIETATIBUS LITTERARUM

SERIES MINOR

1. TREVOR EATON: *The Semantics of Literature*. 1966. 72 pp.
Gld. 9.–

2. WALTER A. KOCH: *Recurrence and a Three-Modal Approach to Poetry*. 1966. 57 pp. Gld. 9.–

SERIES PRACTICA

1. ROBERT G. COHN: *Mallarmé's Masterwork: New Findings.* 1966. 144 pp. 24 facs. Gld. 20.–

SERIES MAIOR

1. MARCUS B. HESTER: *The Meaning of Poetic Metaphor: An Analysis in the Light of Wittgenstein's Claim that Meaning is Use*. 1967. 230 pp. Gld. 35.–

MOUTON · PUBLISHERS · THE HAGUE